THE
JUVENILE NOVELS
OF
WORLD WAR II

Recent Titles in
Bibliographies and Indexes in World Literature

THE
JUVENILE NOVELS
OF
WORLD WAR II

An Annotated Bibliography

Desmond Taylor

Bibliographies and Indexes in World Literature,
Number 44

GREENWOOD PRESS
Westport, Connecticut • London

Library of Congress Cataloging-in-Publication Data

Taylor, Desmond.
    The juvenile novels of World War II : an annotated bibliography /
Desmond Taylor.
       p.   cm.—(Bibliographies and indexes in world literature,
ISSN 0742-6801 ; no. 44)
      ISBN 0-313-29194-2
      1. Children's stories—Bibliography. 2. Young adult fiction—
Bibliography. 3. World war, 1939-1945—Juvenile fiction—
Bibliography. I. Title. II. Series.
Z1037.T26   1994   94-16071

British Library Cataloguing in Publication Data is available.

Library of Congress Catalog Card Number: 94-16071
ISBN: 0-313-29194-2
ISSN: 0742-6801

First published in 1994

Greenwood Press, 88 Post Road West, Westport, CT 06881
An imprint of Greenwood Publishing Group, Inc.

Printed in the United States of America

∞™

The paper used in this book complies with the
Permanent Paper Standard issued by the National
Information Standards Organization (Z39.48-1984).

10 9 8 7 6 5 4 3 2 1

To Alexandria, my granddaughter,

"May you never need to live through it."

To Ingeborg, my dearest wife,

who lived through it as a child in Rosenheim.

CONTENTS

PREFACE

This annotated bibliography of World War II juvenile novels completes the larger project of the author to identify all of the novels about World War II. The adult novels were covered in *The Novels of World War II, an Annotated Bibliography* (New York: 1993. Two volumes). Thus, these 438 juvenile novels about World War II are an indispensable element of the total picture of the Second World War. Indeed, considered with the earlier World War I bibliography, *The Novels of World War I, an Annotated Bibliography* (New York: 1981. 513 p.) which included both juvenile and adult titles, it is now possible for the first time to view the complete array of world war novels and develop an informed impression of just how these two great world wars affected children and adults throughout the world, in combat, on the homefront, in the concentration camps and ghettos, and in a number of unexpected circumstances and places.

Consequently, for the serious student of the world war novel, all of these bibliographies can be considered as integral parts of a much larger work which explores the world war novels of the twentieth century. How the great wars are viewed through the novel, both juvenile and adult, and what plots and topics were deemed sufficiently important to appeal to readers of all ages, constitute a reality that may be far more accurate than imagined. Consider these words of Gerald Brenan: "You can't get at the truth by writing history; you can only get at it through novels."

Only juvenile novels in English or translated into English are included. If a title is bound separately, it is considered an independent work and included. The entries are arranged chronologically by year and then alphabetically by last name of author within their year of publication. No effort has been made to include picture books; the emphasis is on narrative and language, although some are listed when especially outstanding, e.g., *Hiroshima No Pika* (1982: J356). Excluded are collections of short stories and non-fiction of any type. Only juvenile novels that use the Second World War as a substantial part of the action or use the war as background are included. No effort was made to list titles that show the effect of the war on postwar life and activities, e.g., refugees, postwar country occupations, war crime trials and criminals, etc.

In the search for all relevant novels to include, standard lists, indexes and bibliographies were checked: the H.W. Wilson *Children's Catalog* and *Fiction Catalog, Cumulated Fiction Index*, 1945-date, critical and historical literary monographs and periodicals such as *Booklist, Bulletin of the Center for Children's Books, Horn Book, Library Journal, Publishers Weekly, British Book News*, etc. The children's section of the *Saturday Review of Literature* was checked in every issue from 1941 to 1949 when several titles were accidentally discovered there that had not turned up through any subject approach. Also specialized book catalogs such as The New York Public Library *Subject Catalog of the World War II Collection* (Boston: G. K. Hall, 1977. Volume two) were carefully examined.

To verify the earliest date and edition of every title listed, all were checked in one or more of the following: *The National Union Catalog, Mansell's, The British Library General Catalogue of Printed Books,* the OCLC and WLN databases, and other sources of authoritative bibliographic information. In cases of simultaneous publication in the U.S. and England, the first publisher indicates the more probable first country of publication. If the book had an earlier imprint than shown in the bibliographic resources, this was judged the most authoritative date. If a title was not available for examination (no matter the information available in reviews or other sources) it is given the "not seen" legend even if an annotation is supplied.

Author, title, and subject indexes are provided for quick and easy reference by any user whether teacher, librarian, parent or child.

For this bibliography I am grateful to those libraries and librarians who graciously loaned their books for this project. The Tacoma Public Library was an especially useful resource.

Faculty typing grant awarded by Associate Dean John Finney was instrumental in preparing the manuscript for publication. Certainly the expert and conscientious word processing and proofing of the text by the capable Grace Mashie has been essential in producing a quality result. Indeed, the encouragement and critique of the introduction and preliminaries by my dearest friend, colleague and man of letters, Johannes Rembert Trigg, is deeply appreciated. It was he who first saw the larger implications of the entire corpus of world war novels on our times and the human condition. All of these people deserve my gratitude and sincere thanks.

Desmond Taylor   Collins Library
Professor   University of Puget Sound
November 1, 1993   Tacoma, Washington

JUVENILE NOVELS OF
WORLD WAR II

INTRODUCTION

Juvenile fiction has tended to be different from most other literature. This observation was particularly true of World War I juvenile stories published for many years after that war, but far less so for World War II juvenile novels beginning with the 1950s. The boys and girls series formula tales emphasizing boy scout virtues and values featured patriotic fervor, belief in God, and the traditional values of honesty, Christian morality, and integrity. World War II children's literature, however, soon saw the beginnings of a less and less parochial American world view, especially by 1960. But with 1939 and through most of the 1940s, it was still the "gee whiz" traditional tried and true formula plot that characterized our response to the Second World War.

The English juvenile series commencing with *Biggles in the Baltic* (1940: J001) and *Worrals of the W.A.A.F.* (1941: J017) which features a woman WAAF officer, continue the traditional approach. In the United States this genre was resuscitated with a vengeance starting with such series as *A Yankee Flier ...* (1941: J006 etc.), *Dave Dawson at ...* (1941: J008 etc.), *Ann Bartlett ...* (1941: J020 etc.), *The Lucky Terrill Flying* stories (1942: J033 etc.), *Kate Russell Wartime Nurse* stories (1942: J044 etc.) and so on through the 1940s and 1950s. Except for the three British children's series about Biggles, Worrals, and Gimlet (1944: J076 etc.) by William Johns, the majority of these juvenile stories in the United States were cranked out by well known series formula writers such as Al Avery (Rutherford Montgomery), Robert Bowen, Ted Copp, Roy Snell, William Starret, etc. in what appropriately qualifies as "gee whiz" heroics along the lines of Tom Swift or Jack Armstrong, "the all American boy," and their female equivalents.

The first title that seems to address the use and status of women in the war, *Sally Wins Her Wings* (1943: J089) by Simmons, traces how a young American woman progresses from civilian pilot training to the RAF Military Ferry Command in 1940 and 1941 in spite of male prejudice. Sally is developed as a character of some depth which is an unusual development in this period. The next advance occurred with *Bars on Her Shoulders* (1943: J093) by Stansbury who fictionalized the story of the first class of women officer candidates trained and commissioned in the U.S. Army Woman's Auxiliary Corps (WAACS). However, this may well have been primarily for recruitment purposes in view of the manpower shortage. It is always amazing what necessity can do to short-sighted policy and regulation. Otherwise, the stories in this and the next decade were typical examples of the traditional formula plots such as *Norma Kent of the WACS* (1943: J090) and *Sally Scott of the WAVES* (1943: J091) both by Roy Snell, and *Nurse Blake Overseas* (1943: J094) by Starret. Feminism and women's rights issues, however, never have received any truly special attention in connection with the juvenile fiction about the Second World War, even in the titles published through 1992. Nonetheless, female characters along with plots and characterizations in general, grew in sophistication and in reality through the years, especially commencing with the 1960s but which, however, does not explain the overwhelming lack of attention to a subject that surely has become of vital concern to all women whether young or old.

A sense of realism about wartime conditions began as early as 1943 with *The Level Land* (J069) and its description of a German attack on a Dutch town. This was followed in 1944 with *Jezebel the Jeep* (J111). Although this story is a lighthearted tale, it introduces a far more real view of combat and war wounds than the standard children's literature of the times. This greater sophistication of subject and treatment begins also to cover refugee stories such as *Twenty and Ten* (1952: J188) by Bishop, the Japanese occupation of China in *To Beat a Tiger* (1953: J190) by Lewis, and heralds the start of a trend in 1956 toward the use of instructional narratives about the war or some aspect such as the people, battle zones, and military occupations, etc. The war itself is now far more authentically portrayed in all its misery and grimness in stories such as *Burma Rifles* (1960: J208) by Bonham which aptly describes Merrill's Marauders in their bloody jungle combat. Indeed, the first really superior novel with high quality writing was *Dangerous Spring* (1961: J211) by Benary which depicts the final days of the war in East Germany and the release of the Buchenwald prisoners. *Gypsy Courier* (1966: J252) by Visser is another thoughtful and intriguing story describing the activities of the Polish underground army in and about Warsaw from May to November of 1944.

The most momentous event of the war was the dropping of the atomic bombs on Japan in 1945. 1962 saw the appearance of the first of only two juvenile stories that deal with the bombing of Hiroshima. *The Day of the Bomb* (J216) by Bruckner provides dramatically accurate descriptions showing the effect of the atomic bomb on the people, the buildings, and the land. The character of Sadako Sasaki has since become an almost mythical figure in Japan for the Japanese regard this character as the Japanese equivalent to Anne Frank. The second title and very likely the more powerful story is the short (only 44 pages) *Hiroshima No Pika* (1982: J356) by Maruki. This has a distinctive and impressive narrative accompanied by a series of stunning illustrations created by the author that vividly reflect the desolation and destruction caused by the explosion and the radiation. This book occupies a singular place in the juvenile literature of the Second World War.

By this time the standard "gee whiz" formula plots and tales so characteristic of juvenile fiction from earlier years had declined substantially in numbers. They have been replaced with more sophisticated and emotionally mature treatments showing the complexity and grays of life rather than just in black and white terms. There is less and less reluctance to tell about the tragic consequences of the war to fathers, brothers, mothers, sisters, and other relatives who are killed by bombs or unfortunate accidents as in *Enemy in the Sky* (1964: J233) by Hilton; or the tensions and fears of daily life in a German occupied country as in *The School with a Difference* (1964: J236) by Meynier, or the panic and hysteria of refugee children before the Dunkirk retreat, *The Long Escape* (1964: J239) by Werstein.

Strangely enough, there are unusually good descriptions of Philippine jungle warfare in *Matt Quarterhill, Rifleman* (1965: J241) by Chamberlain which could very well be of interest to some adult readers. This author has also written the first story featuring the effectiveness of an American Indian in combat and in military leadership with *Murphy Higheagle, Paratrooper* (1966: J247) set in French hedgerow country. *Star of Danger* (1966: J249) by Levin depicts the fate of two Jewish boys in Denmark when the Nazis begin their program to send all Danish Jews to concentration camps. This is an especially realistic and well written account about the activities of the Danish underground at all levels. A day-to-day account of the actions of the French Resistance is realistically albeit dramatically described in the thriller *The Dangerous Game* (1977: J322) by Dank. For a frank picture of the misery and chaos brought on the German civilians by National Socialist policies and the Allied bombings see *Darkness over the Land* (1966: J251) by Stiles.

On the other hand, a sad and poignant story about the pitiful street children of Naples and their search for a real family, a real home, somewhere, someplace, someday, is sensitively recounted in *The Little Fishes* (1967: J258) by Haugaard. The anti-war theme is effectively introduced in *His Enemy, His Friend* (1967: J260) by Tunis in showing the futility of hatred and revenge during the occupation of France and in the postwar world. A forthright, aptly conceived and well written tale that exposes the true nature of the resistance underground war in occupied Norway is grimly described in *The Fight in the Mountains* (1968: J264) by Bernhardsen. This is also true of *A Fall from Aloft* (1968: J266) by Burland which perceptively explores the traumatic coming of age of an English thirteen-year-old boy while on a wartime convoy journey. The sea voyage in particular is realistically described in considerable detail and with no mincing of words even about the natural functions of the human body.

There are only two juvenile stories that deal with the nature and/or lot of blacks during the war. (For adult novels on this subject consult the Introduction to my recent book: *Novels of World War II: An Annotated Bibliography*. New York: 1993 in 2 volumes.) *Black Soldier* (1968: J268) by Clarke is an honest and forthright story covering race prejudice in the U.S. Army. The black protagonist is depicted through basic training, and overseas in England and in battle in Europe. He is eager to fight for his country but is invariably subjected to discrimination and segregation policies even in such battles as the D-Day invasion and the Battle of the Bulge. *The Cay* (1969: J275) by Taylor deals with an eleven-year-old boy who is saved by a large, ugly old black when their freighter is torpedoed. The young boy has all the racial prejudices of his short life dispelled under the gentle and considerate care of the old West Indian. The racial theme, however, is presented in such a natural and unobtrusive manner that there is no sense of sermonizing; rather only an avuncular relationship between the boy and the older man, human to human, beyond race, or culture.

The city of London during the Blitz is a frequent background or primary setting for a good many juvenile novels. *Fireweed* (1969: J277) by Walsh and *Dawn of Fear* (1970: J278) by Cooper are two typical titles that capitalize on this setting. In addition, stories describing the disillusionment of the young in Germany with the Nazi regime such as *Never to be Free* (1970: J279) by Grund, occur with increasing frequency. By 1970, there are more and more story examples depicting the true reality of war: from bombings to the death and murder of innocent children and adults; and the cruel and inhuman treatment in the holocaust camps from the perspective of East European and Russian child protagonists.

Children's fiction by now has embraced the point of view of many nationalities other than just the American, English, Dutch or French. The other European nationalities, German, Russian, African, and the peoples of the Far East and Japan are clearly in evidence although the American and European perspective is clearly the dominant one. Children's fiction has by now shown the impact of the war everywhere, from the actual battle zones to the home fronts whether in America, England, Australia, or Singapore, Japan, and China. By and large, World War II juvenile stories reflect increasingly accurate representations of the perceptions and worlds of children as they encounter the war and its effects on their daily lives. For example, *Code: Polonaise* (1971: J287) by Wuorio is an excellent example that also uses Polish refugee children to show the committed resolve of the resistance movement to deal realistically and directly with the more ghastly aspects of the wartime atrocities in Poland.

As a consequence, there are more and more examples of holocaust concentration camp stories that begin in any one of the German occupied countries, e.g., *I am Rosemarie* (1972: J288) by Moskin is placed initially in occupied Holland. Lustig puts his powerful short novel *Darkness Casts No Shadow* (1976: J320) in the Terezin camp just outside Prague. (Although this is a narrative that may qualify more as an adult story, it nonetheless deserves an honored place in children's literature.) For a superior fantasy time-machine approach, *The Devil's Arithmetic* (1988: J391) by Yolen bears wrenching witness to the concentration camp horrors in Poland as borne by Jewish villagers. A sophisticated story that wrestles with the good and evil Janus character of the human self is placed in occupied Warsaw in *The Man from the Other Side* (1991: J425) by Orlev. Also there is occasionally a story that honestly describes the German (not Nazi) point of view about a Jewish family such as in the Netherlands in *The Borrowed House* (1975: J313) by Van Stockum.

However, this is not to imply that examples of the typical wartime animal story are lacking. The war dog tale is the most frequent and begins with *Renni the Rescuer* (1940: J004), and continues with *AWOL K-9 Commando* (1944: J135), *Unleash the Dogs of War* (1944: J139), and *Short Leash* (1945: J163), but *Bel Ria* (1977: J321) by Burnford, in contrast with the war dog plots of others, traces the sentimental wanderings of a small dog in France and England. The most unusual animal story is the sad *Poor Elephants* (1979: J340) by Tsuchiya which covers the forced deaths by starvation of all the elephants in the Tokyo zoo when their food can no longer be obtained during the war.

For the first time, the Soviet Secret Police (NKVD) is depicted as an evil force equivalent to the Gestapo in *Edge of Darkness* (1979: J335) by Gessner. This is an almost unbelievable story about terrorist activities in Latvia. Probably the most powerful holocaust story is *Gideon* (1981: J347) by Aaron. This is a narrative that bluntly describes concentration camp conditions and atrocities in such realistic and horrible detail that even some adults might find this narrative rather strong stuff to handle.

There were only six stories about the treatment and detention of Japanese-Americans on the West Coast. The first, *The Moved Outers* (1945: J159) by Means, about the Ohara Japanese family that is sent to a relocation camp near the west coast after Pearl Harbor, is a factually based and dramatic account. The second title, *Tradition* (1946: J172), describes the reception and eventual acceptance of two Nisei teenagers in a Chicago suburb. Most of the emphasis seems to be on teenage social life and school. *Journey to Topaz* (1971: J286) by Uchida is an eloquent account of the bewilderment and loss that many Japanese-Americans experienced at a war relocation center in Utah.

Aloha Means Come Back (1991: J420) is placed in Hawaii and shows the suspicions too many Americans had even in multicultural Hawaii. On the other hand, the multicultural tolerance of Hawaiians compared to that of West Coast Americans is dramatically exposed in *Pearl Harbor is Burning!* (1991: J421) by Kudlinski. The sixth and last narrative, *The Moon Bridge* (1992: J438) by Savin, is placed in a San Francisco school where prejudice is widespread, but a friendship between two girls survives their separation to the end of the war.

A more lighthearted story occasionally begins to appear by 1983. Set mainly on the American home front and directed at younger children, *Eddie Spaghetti on the Home Front* (1983: J361) by Frascino tends to typify this fictional approach to wartime. The American Girls Collection series published from 1986 through 1988 (J375, J376, J377, J381, and J390) by Tripp continues to capitalize on home front life in these tales for young girls. Nonetheless, most of the juvenile literature continues the trend to educate children on the actual reality of wartime, whether back home, in resistance activities, in the military services and battle, or otherwise. In one case, *Escape from the Holocaust* (1985: J370) by Roseman, a bizarre game approach is seriously presented. The narrative gives the young reader options, each with its own consequences that demand further choices as the young reader imaginatively struggles to survive extermination in the death camps. With the defeat of the Third Reich, the young reader learns what life will be like if one chooses to live in Israel, America, or some European country. An unusual story that captures the desperate refugee circumstances of two young Japanese girls and their mother stranded in Korea is described in *So Far From the Bamboo Grove* (1986: J378) by Watkins. There is no other juvenile novel that features this theme and this particular Japanese point of view.

In the final examples, the wanderings of young preadolescent boys chart the desperate treks and wartime experiences of very young children. *Along the Tracks* (1991: J415) by Bergman sensitively traces the travels of Yankele, an eight-year-old Jewish boy, in Russia and Poland over four years in search of his mother. The other tale with a similar plot is *We Were Not Like Other People* (1989: J400) by Sevela which is about a nameless Soviet Jewish boy whose father disappears in one of the purges of Stalin. He describes his years of nightmarish wandering from the age of nine in 1937 on to 1946 which include an almost starving incarceration with extremely hazardous machinery in a Russian vocational school, a stint as a forced farm laborer in Siberia, and battle experiences on the German-Russian front. Written with a sensitive and individual prose style, the translation is outstanding while the narrative exhibits an impressive no "kid gloves" realism.

It is interesting to compare the number of juvenile stories about the two world wars. Over 370 titles had appeared by 1980 about the First World War while over 438 have been published through 1992 on the Second World War. The years of the largest number published about World War II are:

1941	21
1942	31
1943	42
1945	25

Never again were more than 10 titles published in a single year (except 17 in 1991), with most of the years from 1946 through 1992 numbering less, far less than ten titles per year except 11 in 1946 and 12 in 1964 and 1990. Thus, it was not so much the number of tales written and published but rather the switch in approach and the greater sophistication in representing the effects of war that has characterized the juvenile novels about the Second World War.

BIBLIOGRAPHY

1940

J001 Johns, W[illiam] E[arl]. *Biggles in the Baltic; A Tale of the Second Great War*. London: Oxford University Press, 1940. 248p.

The plot continues the adventures of RAF Major James Bigglesworth and his crew as they receive a special assignment to the Baltic sea. They are to man a secret base on a tiny uninhabited island from where they can harass and possibly destroy German shipping as well as other enemy military activities. The men manage to hold out against the German navy for much longer than they anticipated and end up responsible for the destruction of a German ammunition dump and marine stores depot, as well as disrupting enemy lines of communications and sinking a host of German naval vessels. At the end they also manage to obtain the current enemy naval code before being airlifted from the island by the RAF and flown home. Suffice it to say that this is a juvenile story heavy on the prowess of the men.

J002 Johns, William Earl. *Biggles in the South Seas*. London: Oxford University Press, 1940. 255p.

Not seen.

J003 Johns, William Earl. *Biggles Secret Agent*. London: Oxford University Press, 1940. 255p.

Biggles on a mission to Finland. Not seen.

J004 Salten, Felix. *Renni the Rescuer; A Dog of the Battlefield*. Translated by Kenneth C. Kaufman. Indianapolis: Bobbs,

Merrill, 1940. 326p. [*Renni der Retter; Das Leben Kriegshundes*. Zurich: A Müller, 1940? 235p.]

It is not quite clear which war is described. All the war descriptions are so vague that the various events and battlefield activities could well have been modeled on the First World War (as the illustrations seem to indicate). In any case, this is a story for children extolling the noble nature of dogs especially the police dog, Renni. Most of the book deals with the proper philosophy, treatment and training of dogs with Renni and his master, George, as the prime focus--at home, on military maneuvers, and on the battlefield. Renni and his master both eventually end up in the army "Sanitary Corps" or special Red Cross unit that rescues the wounded from the battlefield. Only of interest to young children, the story is by the author of the classic "Bambi" animal tale.

J005   Van Gelder, Robert. *The Enemy in the House*. New York: Dial Press, 1940. 223p.

A facile mystery tale for boys about Slappy, a young reporter, who goes through a thirty-six-hour whirlwind of activity that results in his exposure of a large gang of Fifth Columnists on the very day the U.S. President arrives in town.

1941

J006   Avery, Al (pseud.) [Rutherford George Montgomery]. *A Yankee Flier with the R.A.F.* New York: Grosset and Dunlap, 1941. 214p.

This is the first title in a gee whiz juvenile series which is reminiscent of many of the serial juvenile novels based on World War I. Stan Wilson is an American posing as a Canadian pilot in the R.A.F. Wilson develops his close friendships with Allison and O'Malley after many joint sorties against German Messerschmitts, Heinkels and Stukas. These three characters and their R.A.F. adventures form the nucleus of all the titles in this series. The heart of this story concerns the efforts of the traitorous Lt. Garret to discredit Wilson and turn invaluable aircraft drawings and strategic information over to the Nazis. Of course, everything turns out smashingly for the three friends by the end.

J007   Barne, Kitty. *May I Keep Dogs?* London: Hamish Hamilton, 1941. 294p.

The 1943 *Saturday Review* notice described this as "an English war story filled with valiant young people and kennel doings." Not seen.

J008   Bowen, Robert Sidney. *Dave Dawson at Dunkirk*. Akron: Saalfield, 1941. 251p.

This is the first title in the Dave Dawson War Adventure series. It is May of 1940 and seventeen-year-old Dave and his father fly to France for a personal tour of the Maginot Line. His father suddenly leaves Dave in France for a meeting in London while Dave is caught by the German invasion. He meets for the first time the English boy Freddy Farmer and they both end up captured by the Germans. They later escape, of course, from jail and steal a German plane only to crash-land in Belgium. They link up with Belgian troops and make their way to Dunkirk where they manage to find a boat and end up safe in London. This is clearly a juvenile series modeled on the plethora of World War I adventure series for boys. Single-dimensional, black and white in characterization and content, this is simplistic entertainment fiction for young readers.

J009   Bowen, Robert Sidney. *Dave Dawson, Flight Lieutenant*. Akron: Saalfield, 1941. 255p.

This is the fifth story in this juvenile series that describes the adventures of Dave Dawson and Freddy Farmer, flight officers in the RAF. This time the two chums are sent on a special mission to scout a secret German defense area on the coast of France that is allegedly designed to prevent the Allied invasion of Europe when the Germans invade Russia. This is all set in motion when a lone enemy Messerschmitt drops the body of a dead British agent over England. The two boys and a third RAF pilot take off on a reconnaissance mission over the mysterious enemy zone when ten English bombers suddenly disappear in the zone. The ploy of the young heroes fails and the Germans manage to force Dave and Freddy to crash-land where they are captured. The boys soon learn, however, the secret of the zone, escape in two enemy aircraft and after the usual and typical daring flight heroics return to England and pull the plug on the infamous German General Von Peiplow and his forces.

J010   Bowen, Robert Sidney. *Dave Dawson in Libya*. Akron: Saalfield, 1941. 252p.

This is the third title in this war series for boys. The two
young pilot heroes of the RAF are now attached to the Fleet
Air Arm in the Mediterranean on a special photo
reconnaissance mission to scout the forthcoming German-
Italian drive against General Wavell's forces in Libya. Freddy
Farmer, the English hero, and his good buddy, Dave Dawson,
are forced to crash-land in the desert. They trek into the desert
and accidentally discover a secret German outpost. In order to
find out all they can, they decide to let themselves be taken
prisoners. They soon learn the main facts about the coming
German advance to Tobruk. The night before they steal a
Messerschmitt fighter and successfully return to warn the
British. This is another anachronistic "gee whiz" tale modeled
on the plentiful boys series stories about the First World War.

J011   Bowen, Robert Sidney. *Dave Dawson on Convoy Patrol*.
       Akron: Saalfield, 1941. 247p.

RAF Flying Officers Dawson and Farmer are selected by the
British Air Marshal to join a select group of pilots singled out
for secret missions against the Germans. Their first assignment
results in their being shot down by an English plane in the
vicinity of an enemy U-boat in the English Channel. When a
British flying boat lands to rescue the two heroes, the U-boat
attempts to torpedo the plane. Thus, begins a series of special
missions all bedeviled by the mysterious Nazi secret agent,
Baron von Khole, who seems to be everywhere. Naturally, the
devious Baron and his flotilla of U-boats are intent on sinking
the life line of Allied ships carrying supplies to England
through the North Atlantic. But the Nazis are foiled in the end
by our two young aces when they take the Baron prisoner and
save the convoy. This is number four in this juvenile *War
Adventure* series.

J012   Bowen, Robert Sidney. *Dave Dawson with the RAF*. Akron:
       Saalfield, 1941. 252p.

This is the second title in the author's *War Adventure* series
of boys' stories. Dave and his English buddy, Freddy Farmer,
are invincible and fearless seventeen-year-old officer pilots.
They have already had their share of dog fights against the
Germans when called to London during a night bombing attack
and given a secret mission to find out the precise day and time
of the German invasion. They are flown to Belgium where they
parachute over Antwerp in an effort to contact their secret
Belgian agent. Suffice it to say, they become separated, are
captured, escape, impersonate German officers, steal a German

aircraft and return to England, etc. and successfully complete their hazardous mission with typical patriotic zeal and enthusiasm. This is a simple formula juvenile story for boys.

J013 Copp, Ted [Theodore B.F. Copp]. *The Bridge of Bombers.* Grosset and Dunlap, 1941. 212p.

This title continues the exploits of Steve Knight, whose latest adventure concerns ferrying bombers from Canada to England. His past exemplary deeds have brought him to the attention of Major Sears, who wants to enlist Steve in the "bridge of bombers." A secondary assignment is to discover why so many B-24s have disappeared during the ferrying. On reaching Montreal and meeting his crew, Steve and the crew are immediately sent out over the Atlantic in an unarmed B-24. The men realize they are being followed and when an engine quits on the B-24 and they crash-land in the water, they are captured and taken aboard a Nazi spy ship disguised as a fishing boat. Naturally, Steve and his crew escape, but only to be arrested by the Canadians for treason. But later they are used to capture the Nazi spy responsible for the disappearance of the B-24s. Ho, hum; another juvenile gee whiz tale.

J014 Copp, Ted [Theodore B.F. Copp]. *The Mystery of Devil's Hand.* New York: Grosset and Dunlap, 1941. 214p.

A Steve Knight Flying story. Not seen.

J015 Johns, William Earl. *Biggles Defies the Swastika.* London: Oxford University Press, 1941. 249p.

Biggles is sent on a secret mission to Norway and becomes involved in the German invasion. Not seen.

J016 Johns, William Earl. *Biggles Hits the Trail.* London: Oxford University Press, 1941. 160p.

Not seen.

J017 Johns, William Earl. *Biggles Sees it Through.* London: Oxford University Press, 1941. 254p.

Biggles joins the RAF. Not seen.

J018 Johns, William Earl. *Spitfire Parade; Stories of Biggles in War-time.* London: Oxford University Press, 1941. 256p.

Describes the adventures of Biggles with the RAF 266 Squadron in the Battle of Britain. Not seen.

J019   Johns, William Earl. *Worrals of the W.A.A.F.* London: Lutterworth, 1941. 219p.

The further adventures of a woman WAAF officer. Not seen.

J020   Johnson, Martha (pseud.) [Elisabeth Carleton Hubbard Lansing]. *Ann Bartlett in the South Pacific.* New York: Thomas Y. Crowell, 1941. 321p.

This story relates the further adventures of the young American nurse after she has escaped from the Philippines to the relative safety of Australia in 1943. Stationed at a base hospital in Sydney, she is anxious to return to front-line duty. She gets her wish when she is sent to a hospital unit in Port Darwin which comes under attack by the Japanese. When volunteers are requested to help locate an American general downed in New Guinea, Ann volunteers. In turn, her plane is destroyed in a tropical storm after Ann and the two pilots parachute into the jungle. They eventually find their way to the coast after weeks of walking and run into Ann's fiancé who has survived for months in the jungle. Together the group is rescued by an American plane. This is the first title of the *Ann Bartlett* series.

J021   Lebeck, Oskar and Gaylord DuBois. *Stratosphere Jim and His Flying Fortress.* New York: Grosset and Dunlap, 1941. 215p.

Jim Baxter, the master designer for the International Aircraft Syndicate, and Harry Wells, a test pilot, are involved with a "stratosphere flying fortress." An unusual mixture of rocket fuel and special engines, make the "flying fortress" capable of reaching 50,000-foot heights and 700-mile-an-hour speeds. The "flying fortress" crew search for war spies in the States but ultimately, in the Atlantic, the "flying fortress" was able to rescue the tanker, *Albatross*, which had been attacked by two submarines. One torpedo had struck the *Albatross* amidships and set the tanker afire, the *Albatross* crew are saved by the men of the "flying fortress."

J022   Maclean, Catherine Macdonald. *Seven for Cordelia.* London: Chambers, 1941. 279p.

This is the first of three stories which describe the experiences of slum children from Edinburgh and Glasgow who are evacuated to a farm in the Scottish highlands. Narrated by a friend of Cordelia Kinross, the tale shows how the children react to the hard work and routine of country life--the seeding and harvesting, but especially the animals. A portion of the story relates the return of the narrator to London where Cordelia's niece is a nurse in a London hospital and is subject to the shock and terror of the September 1940 blitz, and eventually killed. The main emphasis, however, is on the farm and the activities of the seven children. The sequels are *Three for Cordelia* (1943) item J83, and *Farewell to Tharrus* (1944) item J125.

J023 Nathan, Robert [Gruntal]. *They Went on Together*. New York: Knopf, 1941. 191p.

A short novel from the perspective of children concerning their forced evacuation (and refugee status) during the war. There are four primary characters: Paul, a young boy, Marie Rose, his very young sister, his mother, and Sylvie, a homeless waif who is adopted by Paul and his mother. Air attacks force the four to leave the security of their home in a wandering quest for safety. Presumedly this is World War II but the dialogue and place names used seem to give an impression of a location in the United States rather than somewhere in Europe or even England. In spite of the subject, the story is too obviously contrived to be convincing to any modern reader.

J024 Travers, P[amela] L[yndon]. *I Go By Sea, I Go By Land*. London: Peter Davies, 1941. 207p.; New York, London: Harper, 1941. 233p.

This is a fictional diary based on actual children and the events of World War II. Sabrina Lind, an eleven-year-old English girl and her younger brother James are sent from England to America when the German bombing raids become a threat to their country home. The diary is composed of the impressions and travel experiences of a young girl in wartime. A view of homefront activities and events from the point of view and interest of a young girl, both in England and in America. Chiefly of interest to juveniles.

J025 Treadgold, Mary. *Left Till Called For*. Garden City, New York: Doubleday, Doran, 1941. 304p.

When the British evacuate the Channel Islands in anticipation of the forthcoming German occupation, two English children are accidentally left behind. Mick and Caroline demonstrate a hardy spirit and special English resourcefulness when they obtain valuable information of interest to the British Secret Service. Mick is even able to decipher a German military code! Their exciting adventures have a happy resolution when they are finally rescued at the end. This is a relatively unsophisticated and straightforward spy tale for adolescents.

J026   Westerman, Percy. *Sea Scouts at Dunkirk*. London: Blackie, 1941. 206p.

The scouts help out with the evacuation of British troops back to England. Not seen.

1942

J027   Avery, Al (pseud.) [Rutherford George Montgomery]. *A Yankee Flier in the Far East*. New York: Grosset and Dunlap, 1942. 216p.

Our three intrepid buddies are assigned to the RAF Near East command for the Singapore campaign in early 1941. Stan Wilson gets most of the star billing while aided and supported by his two friends, O'Malley and Allison. The evil traitor is Colonel Munson who turns out to be a Nazi spy in cahoots with the Japanese forces. The three volunteer for the Chinese air force under Chiang Kai-shek and are sent to defend the Rangoon area. Stan crash-lands and is taken prisoner in Siam where he escapes with the aid of a Burmese girl. The feature action occurs when they all return to bomb the secret Japanese jungle airfield and rescue the Thai girl who aided Wilson to escape. As is typical in these black and white juvenile war stories, the three heroes can do no wrong while the enemy is treacherous and scarcely human. This is the second title in this *Yankee Flier* series.

J028   Bechdolt, Jack [John Ernest Bechdolt]. *Junior Air Raid Wardens*. Philadelphia: Lippincott, 1942. 175p.

This is a homefront civil defense tale placed on the east coast of the United States which resonably well captures the wartime flavor of those times, i.e., blackouts, U-boat attacks, etc. The story follows two young boys, Greg Rowan, sixteen-years-old, and Ben Cuyler, seventeen-years-old, as they become junior air raid wardens and help foil a German spy at work in their communmity. There are the usual dramatic elements that supposedly appeal to pre-adolescent readers. Indeed, there is even a strong defense by the boys in favor of justice for their ethnic friend Tony when enemy war hysteria afflicts some of their friends and neighbors.

J029   Bowen, Robert Sidney. *Dave Dawson at Singapore*. Akron: Saalfield, 1942. 250p.

The two chums in this war adventure series are the English Freddy Farmer and the American Dave Dawson. Both are ace pilots in the RAF. Dawson has requested their transfer to the Far East Fleet Air Arm in Singapore where they are heading as the story begins. The action occurs during 1940 and 1941. The boys are soon involved in air surveillance over the China Sea where they are shot down by a Jap sub. This leads to Nazi spies at the Devil's Den in Singapore on Bukum Street, "the street of a million different smells." The two intrepid aces end up posing as Luftwaffe pilots sent by the evil Serrangi on an intelligence mission to a Japanese general who reveals his plan to attack Singapore momentarily. The action ends with the Japanese attack on Pearl Harbor and the official entrance of the U.S. into the war.

J030   Bowen, Robert Sidney. *Dave Dawson with the Air Corps*. Akron: Saalfield, 1942. 251p.; New York: Crown, 1942. 251p.

Dave and Freddy continue their intelligence work for Colonel Welsh. They meet him in Oakland, California for their new mission. While waiting for the arrival of the Colonel, they take a recreational plane ride and discover a newly crashed plane in the nearby mountains. They rescue the pilot who dies after imparting a cryptic message about the Axis spy "seven-eleven." They then are sent to the Albuquerque air base on the trail of spies. More mysteries and strange events occur before their departure to Texas and finally their arrival in the Canal Zone where they suspect a Nazi attack on the Panama Canal. They discover a secret German base in the Caribbean but are tricked and captured. Naturally, they escape, destroy the base with a bomb and head back to the Canal Zone flushed with gleeful success. This is the eighth story in the juvenile *War Adventure* series.

J031   Bowen, R[obert] Sidney. *Dave Dawson with the Commandos*. Akron: Saalfield, 1942. 248p.

This juvenile tale introduces the further daring exploits of the two war aces, American pilot Dave Dawson and English pilot Freddy Farmer as they accept the challenge of Major Barber to kidnap and bring to England the two top German generals responsible for Nazi crimes against mankind. Against almost impossible odds the two young officers carry out their mission with typical derring-do.

J032   Bowen, Robert Sidney. *Dave Dawson with the Pacific Fleet*. Akron: Saalfield, 1942. 249p.

Dave and his English chum are on loan from the RAF to U.S. Intelligence. They arrive in New York City and are sent to meet Colonel Welsh, Chief of U.S. Military Intelligence. Their assignment is to catch traitors in the U.S. Army and Navy. The first mission is to join the pilot crew on the aircraft carrier *Indian*. They and Welsh fly through the southern states but are shot down by a mysterious aircraft. Suffice it to say that they manage to escape and join the carrier crew minutes before it leaves San Diego for the Pacific. Dave and Freddy soon detect traitors in their flying group as they attempt to make contact with a Japanese warship. This is the seventh story in the *War Adventure* series for juveniles.

J033   Cook, Canfield. *Sky Attack*. New York: Grosset and Dunlap, 1942. 215p.

This is the second title in the *Lucky Terrell Flying Story* series for boys. American Bob Terrell is a Flying Officer in the RAF. The plot promptly begins with a dramatic escape of the wounded Terrell in France when he steals a Messerschmitt and flies back to England. After a quick hospital recovery he and his two buddies, Eric Prentiss and Don White, transfer from their fighter squadron to the Bomber Command where they will fly a new type, high altitude bomber, the Stratohawk. Terrell meets a new pilot who joins his group as the third buddy. Their first bomber mission is to a north German naval base. Another is a mission to Hamburg followed by an emergency landing just behind the Russian lines in the east. Suffice it to say that Bob foils a sabotage attempt at his base in Scotland, wins out over the wily Jerries, and concludes a successful European tour of duty by being transferred with his buddies to the Far East. Simplistic, fast action and heroism at every turn are some of the formula techniques in this typical boys' series.

J034   Cook, Canfield. *Spitfire Pilot*. New York: Grosset and Dunlap, 1942. 209p.

This is another of the few anachronistic boys' series stories lingering on into the Second World War era. Bob or "Lucky" Terrell is the Texas hero who performs wondrous and brave exploits in the air war against the Nazi enemy on behalf of the Allies, and in this case the English. Lucky and his American buddies are exemplars of the gee whiz American boy that for so long served as models for the younger generation. Bob and his air force friends accompany Eric, their English pilot buddy, to England where they are soon flying the Spitfire fighter. Bob is shot down over Germany and is taken as a POW, but manages in short order to steal a Messerschmitt and escape back to England! This is the first of the *Lucky Terrell Flying Stories*.

J035 Copp, Ted [Theodore B.F. Copp]. *The Phantom Fleet*. New York: Grosset and Dunlap, 1942. 213p.

Not seen.

J036 Dalgliesh, Alice. *Gulliver Joins the Army*. New York: Scribner, 1942. 93 p.

About half of this narrative takes place after Pearl Harbor. The Majolica family has acquired so many pets that they have moved to a farm in Connecticut. Gulliver, a German Shepherd dog, is the special pet of Tony, the son. When Tony goes off to war, Gulliver is patriotically sent to the Dogs for Defense, Inc. as another family contribution to the war effort. The story concludes when Tony and Gulliver, both in the army, briefly meet in England on their way to their permanent war assignments. The story is a warm, homey picture of family life with a dog as the special central character. There is plenty of emphasis on conservation, Red Cross work, and patriotic duty as an American citizen.

J037 Deutsch, Babette. *The Welcome*. New York: Harper, 1942. 197 p.

Set in New York City, the exact time is unknown except that German refugees are now in the United States but the Japanese are yet to attack Pearl Harbor. Ernst Keller and his sister Erika have recently come from England. The plot covers the reception of Ernst by American school children, especially thirteen-year-old Thursty. Thursty and Ernst eventually become good friends when Thursty temporarily moves into the Welcome, a club for refugee children, after burglars raid his grandmother's apartment where he has been living. The story has a strong didactic message in support of understanding and tolerance of strangers and foreigners. The plot, dialog and incidents are on the level of pre-adolescent behavior and interests. Although the message is laudable the text seems dated with only limited interest to young readers today.

J038   Flexner, Hortense. *The Wishing Window*. Philadelphia: Frederick A. Stokes, 1942. 63p.

The Germans have invaded France. Two very small village children have had a habit of playing a game of pretend outside the local bakery windows. With the arrival of the Germans, Clare and Jacques all too soon see the distruction of many village buildings, including their favorite bakery. They seize the opportunity to enter the bombed-out shop and discover in the rubble the bread and sweet buns they have never been able to eat before. Shortly, they also encounter Mimi, the bakery cat. Then the bakery delivery boy turns up and leads them into the fields and eventually to their waiting parents. The text is especially constructed for young children.

J039   Haines, Donal Hamilton. *Shadow on the Campus*. New York: Farrar and Rinehart, 1942. 278p.

Strictly speaking, this "college" story about student life on a large Western University campus could be considered prewar since it is placed from the fall of 1939 to November of 1940. The narrative tends to be crammed with all aspects of student life, but the focus is the European war and its impact on young people. A Fifth Column spy plot tends to supplant the usual social, fraternity, and football interests, and helps to focus the attention of the reader on various war related issues: involvement, isolationism, sabotage, profiteering, etc. Michael is the primary student character who decides to leave for action in Europe by the conclusion of the story; well in advance of Pearl Harbor and the American declaration of war. There is more than just an odor of propaganda, especially in the last few chapters. The plot and the dialogue convey a dated earnestness.

J040   Johns, William Earl. *Biggles Sweeps the Desert, A "Biggles" Squadron Story*. London: Hodder and Stoughton, 1942. 208p.

Not seen.

J041   Johns, William Earl. *Sinister Service*. London: Oxford University Press, 1942. 191p.

Not seen.

J042 Johns, William Earl. *Worralls Carries On.* London: Lutterworth, 1942. 142p.

More adventures of Worralls in the WAAF. Not seen.

J043 Johns, William Earl. *Worralls Flies Again.* London: Hodder and Stoughton, 1942. 189p.

Not seen.

J044 Johnson, Martha (pseud.) [Elisabeth Carleton (Hubbard) Lansing]. *Kate Russell Wartime Nurse.* New York: Thomas Y. Crowell, 1942. 257p.

A juvenile tale about Kate Russell, a Red Cross nurse, as she joins the Harvard Red Cross Medical Unit, and leaves the United States for England aboard a convoyed British freighter. After three days at sea near Iceland, the ship is torpedoed and sinks shortly after the passengers and crew enter the lifeboat. Nearly a week adrift, the lifeboat is spotted and the survivors rescued by a friendly destroyer. Naturally, Kate is a tower of strength and a model of resolute and patriotic behavior.

J045 Kalab, Theresa [Theresa (Kalab) Smith]. *Watching for Winkie.* New York: Longmans, Green, 1942. 47p.

A simple story about Winkie, the brave carrier pigeon of young Tommy MacIntosh of Dundee, Scotland. Tommy has been helping Mr. Raymond with the care and watch of special carrier pigeons used by the British government to carry messages during wartime. Tommy believes that his pigeon will be especially good. When Tommy's father who is a pilot in the RAF has his bomber damaged on an offensive patrol over the coast of Norway, Winkie is released by the crew and makes the flight back to Scotland in record time. Thus, Tommy's father and his crew are all saved and Winkie is the hero. Although this may be considered a picture book only nine of the pages of large print text have illustrations.

J046 Lent, Henry B[olles]. *Air Patrol: Jim Brewster Flies For the U.S. Coast Guard.* New York: Macmillan, 1942. 171p.

The plot is based on a close examination of Coast Guard pilots stationed at the Brooklyn Air Station. Ensign Jim Brewster has earned his wings at Pensacola, after having passed the four-year course at the Coast Guard Academy at New London. The narrative covers Jim's routine workday at the station learning to fly J4F-1 Grummans, PBY patrol bombers, and various other aircraft. When the number of ship sinkings along the east coast dramatically increases, Jim is assigned to hunt for German subs. Jim rescues survivors and flies patrol for slow moving freighters. When one is torpedoed, he and his crew bomb the enemy sub to smithereens. Jim, of course, is awarded The Distinguished Flying Cross!

J047   Mallette, Gertrude Ethel. *Inside Out.* Garden City, New York: Doubleday, Doran, 1942. 278p.

Placed during the early war years in New York City, the plot features Linda Sherrill, the young daughter of a physician, who aspires to be an artist. Discouraged by her art teacher, a long illness provides her with the opportunity to pratice sketching moving objects seen through binoculars from her bedroom window. Part of her field of vision is the Hudson River and its military ship traffic. Suffice it to say that her observations reveal a German spy plot in the offing. Clearly a story for young girls, the mixture of art training, spy mystery, and romance is the standard stuff of stories for adolescents. The war serves as a device to support the detective work and to lend an air of national urgency to the proceedings.

J048   McSwigan, Marie. *Snow Treasure.* New York: Dutton, 1942. 178p.

A fictionalized account of an actual incident in German-occupied Norway. A group of Norwegian children manage to carry gold bullion bars down a mountain by riding their sleds past the enemy soldiers. The children hide the gold under their snowmen where adult resistance fighters remove it each night and load it into a nearby freighter which eventually carries the treasure all the way to Baltimore by June 28, 1940. The narrative tends toward black and white characterizations--the courage, wits, and determination of the children and their adult friends against the arrogance and treachery of the Nazi invaders. A good read for nine- to twelve-year-olds.

J049   Montgomery, Rutherford G[eorge] [Al Avery (pseud.)]. *Hurricane Yank.* Philadelphia: David Mckay, 1942. 250p.

Relates the adventures of an American bomber pilot in England during the early years of the war. Kelly Maynard, a former test pilot, arrives in England and promptly joins the

80th RAF Squadron to fly Hurricanes on bombing raids over Germany. The narrative is made up of the daring feats of the young American pilot and his two comrades, Flight Lieutenant Chet Prentiss and a Polish pilot called Mike who had escaped from Poland when his country fell to the Germans in 1939.

J050   Montgomery, Rutherford George [Al Avery (pseud.)]. *Thumbs Up!* Philadelphia: David Mckay, 1942. 256p.

Another fast action juvenile war story about three Marine pilots in the Pacific air war. The conventional plot begins with their air acrobatics and heroics against a Japanese invasion of their Pacific Paris Island. The scene soon moves to the Philippines and the Battle of Bataan. The three Marine heroes, Lts. O'Toole, Rivers and Captain Edwards, engage in what can only be viewed as some prepubescent boy's vision of the war in the air against the nasty Jap. Strictly for undiscriminating boy readers.

J051   Phillips, Ethel Calvert. *Brian's Victory.* Boston: Houghton Mifflin, 1942. 86p.

A short and simple story that begins in wartime England where eleven-year-old Brian lives in a small village. With his father in the British Army in Africa, Brian experiences increasing bombing raids on his village. These reach such an intensity that his mother is once again forced to send him away, this time to America to live with his uncle and aunt. He flies via Lisbon to America. In the Bermuda stopover he is given a small white kitten who he names Victory (hence the title). Once in the states and settled in New Jersey, he is enrolled in school where he makes, of course, many American friends. An endearing boy, he sells his treasured white kitten to raise money for the British-American Ambulance Fund. Selected to perform a native dance with Flora, a Scottish girl in his school, he is first given a jet black kitten called Liberty as a token of his school mates' friendship. The story concludes with Brian and Flora doing their Scottish dance. There is some sense of wartime homefront conditions in England but in America most of the emphasis is on normal everyday life as lived by children, except for Brian, and generally unrelated to the war.

J052   Riesenberg, Felix. *Salvage, A Modern Sea Story.* New York: Dodd, Mead, 1942. 220p.

A juvenile story in which an American freighter encounters a derelict vessel shortly after the Pearl Harbor attack. Before the American crew are able to salvage the vessel they are captured by an enemy raider and boarded. They turn the tables on their Japanese captors and manage to escape only to encounter a severe storm. Afterwards they accidentally enter a battle zone before towing the derelict safely into an American harbor.

J053   Snell, Roy Judson. *Wings for Victory*. Chicago: M.A. Donohue and Company, 1942. 251p.

The action is centered in Hawaii before, during and after the Japanese attack on Pearl Harbor. Red, Billy McFadden, Jane Howe, Jack Darin and their buddies in the U.S. Army Air Force are among the intrepid and patriotic protagonists battling against the sneaky and devious Japs and their spies in Hawaii. There is a goodly taste of spy and counter spy activity as well as air battles against the enemy. This is a formula story stressing action, patriotism, and the blatant evil of the Japs!

J054   Starret, William (pseud.) [Marshall McClintock]. *Nurse Blake, U.S.A.* New York: Gramercy Publishing Company, 1942. 250p.

Not seen.

J055   Watson, Helen Orr. *Top Kick, U.S. Army Horse*. Boston: Houghton Mifflin, 1942. 217p.

First and foremost this is a story for horse lovers. The horse Top Kick is followed from his birth, weaning and training at an Army Remount Depot to other military bases in the States, and finally to his adventures against the Japanese in the Philippines. Just prior to the withdrawal of McArthur to Bataan, the horse saves the life of his master, Lieutenant Bayley. Naturally, the horse is fearless and brave, and a model of devotion and intelligence. The bulk of the narrative is devoted to the training experiences of Top Kick in this country. Only the last 40 pages deal with the war in the Philippines. The text concludes as Bayley and Top Kick leave to join the forces of McArthur on Bataan.

1943

J056 Avery, Al (pseud.) [Robert G. Montgomery]. *A Yankee Flier in North Africa*. New York: Grosset and Dunlap, 1943. 214p.

This is the fourth title in this series. The three intrepid air aces are now in Tunisia. The duty station is a new and remote air field called Mud Flat because of the terribly muddy conditions. Naturally, all three, Allison, Wilson, and O'Malley figure out how to take off and land in spite of the mud and rocks. There are the usual combat air scenes but this time Allison is shot down and his two buddies crash-land to pull him from his burning plane. Since this is behind the German lines, they decide to steal a German tank and slip over the front lines to their side. Of course, they succeed and return to Mud Flat Field and rush back into the war again. Their evil opposition is Fritz Stoner, the German air ace, and his Red Stingers. The rest of the rah, rah, eat 'em up plot consists of how the three heroes manage to shoot down most of the Stingers and capture the arrogant Stoner in spite of disobeying their commander's orders. The only connection to the real war is the occasional use of terms such as Focke-Wulf, Stuka, and P-38.

J057 Avery, Al (pseud.) [Rutherford George Montgomery]. *A Yankee Flier in the South Pacific*. New York: Grosset and Dunlap, 1943. 208p.

Not seen.

J058 Barne, Kitty. *We'll Meet in England*. New York: Dodd, Mead, 1943. 260p.

When fifteen-year-old Hertha Larson sees a stranded small boat along the fjord near her village in Norway, she immediately believes this is the opportunity for her and her brother to escape from the German occupied country and head for England where they can better help the fight to free Norway. An elderly English seaman assists them to escape and sail his small boat to Scotland. On the way they rescue an exhausted RAF pilot from his rubber life-raft and all four eventually succeed in reaching England. The narrative is filled with the type of adventure and excitement designed to appeal to young readers and demonstrate the patriotism of the Norwegians.

J059   Beim, Lorraine and Jerrold. *Igor's Summer: a story of our Russian Friends*. New York: Russian War Relief, Inc., 1943. 59p.

This is a story about a Russian army doctor's son and his wartime activities and everyday life. Igor is eleven-years-old and eager to hear from his father at the front while he goes to school in Moscow. Igor is constantly casting about to find ways and projects to help the war effort such as gardening, crop harvesting, and volunteering to work on the local farms along with other Russian children. This is a simple story designed to encourage American support for the Russian war effort but especially for Russian children. The last page is a cut-out addressed to "Dear Russian Friend" in an effort to encourage the child reader to write a supportive note to Russia.

J060   Berger, Josef. *Subchaser Jim*. Boston: Little, Brown, 1943. 302p.

The hero is eighteen-year-old Jim Ellis who is the skipper of his own fishing schooner based in Gloucester, Massachusetts. The plot abounds with German spies and mysterious goings-on both with Jim's fishing crew and other fishing boats. When the war begins on page 199 with the Japanese attack on Pearl Harbor, Jim and his companions have already been at work for Naval Intelligence by tracking and destroying German subs off the coast of Cape Cod. Jim is now commissioned an Ensign and his schooner is fitted with torpedoes to entrap German U-boats. By the end of this adventure several subs have been destroyed before Jim's fishing boat is sunk. But Jim and his crew are all safe while the Navy announces that Jim will get a new boat.

J061   Bowen, Robert Sidney. *Dave Dawson on Guadalcanal*. Akron: Saalfield, 1943. 246p.; New York: Crown, 1943. 246p.

Our two flying aces are now headed to Australia from India. They reach Sydney and have a surprise visit from Colonel Welsh who informs them of their next mission, a "flight to nowhere" via a destroyer headed for a rendezvous with a carrier task force headed for a surprise attack on the Solomon Islands. Dave and Freddy have the mission to locate at all costs the enemy invasion force so they can be turned back or prevented from interfering with the Guadalcanal surprise attack. The two heroes are shot down, take to their life raft but are picked up by a Nazi sub. They learn of the whereabouts of Admiral Sasebo and his carrier force before being transferred to an enemy carrier for questioning. They are permitted to escape in a Japanese plane which the enemy hopes will lead them to the location of the U.S. Naval Task Force. Suffice it to say that the two aces quickly catch on to this nefarious scheme, destroy three zeros trailing them and accidentally run into their own naval task force where Dave is sent to sick bay for his wounds. Naturally, everything comes up roses in this twelfth installment of the *War Adventure* series.

J062   Bowen, Robert Sidney. *Dave Dawson with the Flying Tigers*. Akron: Saalfield, 1943. 250p.; New York: Crown, 1943. 250p.

Close pals and expert flying aces, Freddy and Dave plan on a long leave in New York City. Dave carries a secret document for Colonel Welsh but Nazi and Jap agents plot their capture in mid-Atlantic by U-boat. Their plane is shot down and they are captured by the "square-headed, pig-eyed" enemy agents. But the intrepid boys quickly overcome the entire crew and are quickly picked up by an English cruiser and go on to New York and their meeting with Welsh. Their new assignment is to aid Chiang Kai-shek in China. After a stopover in Hawaii and an assassination attempt on them, they travel by carrier and bomber to China. When they are shot down in the Philippines they nevertheless manage to steal an enemy aircraft and reach Flying Tiger air space where they eventually go on to help save over 20,000 troops of Kai-shek. This is the eleventh title of this series and filled with the typical "gee whiz" rhetoric and coincidental actions and heroics.

J063   Brier, Howard M. *Swing Shift*. New York: Random House, 1943. 265p.

The story is placed in Seattle in 1942 where a young farm boy from North Dakota, Dave Marshall, arrives looking for work after Pearl Harbor. He finds a job in the shipyards where he discovers a plot to undermine the shipyard by blowing up the new vessels when they are launched. Both the FBI and the United States Coast Guard become involved. The narrative covers the technical aspects of welding, boilermaking, shipfitting, and all the other activities performed in a shipyard during wartime.

J064   Clements, Eileen Helen. *Cherry Harvest*. London: Hodder and Stoughton, 1943. 223p.

An insignificant homefront romance set at an English girl's school in the Cotswolds. The war and the local scene is viewed through the eyes of the harassed headmistress. During the four-day break between school terms, several members of the RAF arrive for an unexpected visit. By summer time at least one spy has been caught in the little village. This is a low key, slow paced tale of extremely limited appeal.

J065   Cook, Canfield. *Lost Squadron*. New York: Grosset and Dunlap, 1943. 216p.

Describes the further adventures of Flight Lieutenant Robert Terrell of the RAF when he and his crew are posted to India. After discovering a secret Japanese airfield, and bombing it out of commission, Terrell's squadron is assigned to China as an advance guard to help push the Japanese out of Burma and China. Their specific mission is to hold an airfield in China until the army rids the surrounding areas of the Japanese. The mission appears to be a failure when their plane ices up flying over the "hump" and they are forced to an emergency landing. However, in a daring escape, the crew foils the enemy and they arrive at their destination to find the rest of their squadron intact.

J066   Cook, Canfield. *Secret Mission*. New York: Grosset and Dunlap, 1943. 210p.

This is the third Lucky Terrell Flying story about the heroic and daredevil exploits of the Texas flying ace and his buddies, co-pilot Don White, and Sgt. McTavish, navigator and bombardier, all attached to the RAF. The immediate mission is to bomb the oil tanks and naval bases in Nazi-occupied Norway. They next fly their secret bombers on a top-secret mission to Malta, Alexandria and into the Pacific air war against the Japanese. This is the usual melodramatic juvenile tale with invincible "gee whiz" heroics which bear little resemblance to the realities of the actual war.

J067   Cook, Canfield. *Springboard to Tokyo*. New York: Grosset and Dunlap, 1943. 210p.

This is one of those few boys' stories of the Second World War that uses the World War I boys' series genre as a model for its style and plot development. It is one of the *Lucky Terrell Flying* stories featuring RAF pilot Robert Terrell and his air squadron as they range from India to a Chinese air base, and their aircraft carrier-based fighter and bomber missions against the Japanese installations in the Far East. This is typical juvenile war story fare with standard dialogue and flying heroics. The fifth title in the Lucky Terrell Flying series.

J068   Crawford, Phyllis. *Second Shift*. New York: Holt, 1943. 211p.

Here is a juvenile homefront story calculated to encourage girls to do their part for the country in factory war work. The heroine is a girl reporter who decides to become a factory worker as long as the war continues. There is an effort to create suspense and drama about whether the heroine will be able to machine thirty-one or thirty-five lap-racing set-ups, or X number of bearings cleaned and polished, etc. There is some similarity to the Soviet proletarian fiction of the twenties, thirties, and forties.

J069   de Jong, Dola [Jan Hoowij]. *The Level Land*. New York: Scribner, 1943. 176p.

The family of Dutch village physician, Dr. Van Oordt, cannot believe that Holland's quiet way of life is threatened. The narrative pictures the peace and tranquility of the Dutch countryside on the eve of the war with the conditions of the German invasion and bombing. The family soon realize that their village near Amsterdam has no special immunity from the war. The author attempts to provide a convincing description of the German attack on this Dutch village as a means to support the Allied cause. There is a special glossary of war terms introduced into the Dutch language by the Germans during the war.

J070   Deming, Dorothy, R.N. *Penny Marsh and Ginger Lee, Wartime Nurses*. New York: Dodd, Mead, 1943. 236p.

A story about two young nurses, Penny Marsh Bridgeman and Ginger Lee. Penny turns to Red Cross nursing, and serves on the homefront, training nurses' aides. Her husband, a physician, volunteers for the military, and when war is declared, leaves with the Army Medical Corps. Ginger joins the Army nurses, volunteers for overseas duty, and is sent overseas to Bataan to help set up a field hospital. Subsequently she is rescued at Bataan and sent to Australia. One of a series of stories featuring Penny Marsh.

J071   Dubois, Gaylord. *Barry Blake of the Flying Fortress*. Racine: Whitman, 1943. 248p.

One of the titles in the "Fighters for Freedom" series. This tale is about Lieutenant Blake and his feats of derring-do with his B-27 bomber and crew. The action begins at Randolph Field but soon follows Blake and his crew on their raid on Rabaul, then New Guinea, and then various other Japanese installations in the South Pacific.

J072 Felsen, Henry Gregor. *Struggle Is Our Brother.* New York: Dutton, 1943. 220p.

This is a juvenile story about Mikhail, a twelve-year-old Cossack boy who forms a guerrilla band when the Germans invade his village and murder his entire family. He has only one thought--how to serve his country and destroy the enemy. He and his group hide in the forest and harass the Germans. Eventually his guerrillas destroy the local dam which was once the pride and chief source of livelihood for the region. This tale might well be considered a propaganda piece that shows the courage and self-sacrifice of the Russians for their homeland.

J073 Felsen, [Henry] Gregor. *Submarine Sailor.* New York: Dutton, 1943. 208p.

Describes an eleven-week operational cruise aboard an American sub which leaves an Australian port to land an American agent in Sagami Bay in Japan. The agent is a Japanese called Yoshimo, who is to report on the location of concealed Japanese war industries. On the way to Japan the sub destroys half a dozen Japanese destroyers. But when the agent gets his information and is picked up by the American sub, the vessel is surrounded by Japanese war ships. Then when Skipper Hawkins is forced to scuttle his submarine, he attempts to convince his Japanese captors that he and his crew are really Germans. It is possible the story tries to demonstrate the capabilities of an American submarine when it struts its stuff.

J074 Johns, William Earl. *Biggles Fails to Return.* London: Hodder and Stoughton, 1943. 223p.

The plot is set in Vichy France. Not seen.

J075 Johns, William Earl. *Biggles in Borneo: A "Biggles Squadron" Story of the Second Great War.* London: Oxford University Press, 1943. 185p.

This is one of a number of titles in a popular juvenile series for boys in the United Kingdom and in the Commonwealth countries. The featured protagonist is Squadron Leader James Bigglesworth, or Biggles for short. An English prospector in Borneo proposes that the British use his secret airfield to harass the Japanese. His plan is eagerly embraced by Biggles and his superiors. Biggles and his men take three fighter planes and one bomber to Borneo where they proceed to harass the enemy and run reconnaissance trips to evaluate the activities of the enemy. Biggles is assisted by the Punans, a local tribe of headhunters. It is easy to see how this type of adventure tale might appeal to boys, but the action and particulars are of small interest to anyone else.

J076 Johns, W[illiam] E[arl]. *King of the Commandos*. Bickley: University of London Press. 1943. 192p.

The first Gimlet story. Not seen.

J077 Johns, William Earl. *Worrals on the War-Path; A Worrals of the W.A.A.F. Story*. London: Hodder and Stoughton, 1943. 191p.

Not seen.

J078 Johnson, Martha (pseud.) [Elisabeth Carleton (Hubbard) Landing]. *Ann Bartlett at Bataan, the Adventures of a Navy Nurse*. New York: Thomas Y. Crowell, 1943. 328p.

A story for young girls which describes the experiences of Ann Bartlett in Hawaii, Wake Island, and Bataan when she escapes from Japanese imprisonment, and is able to join an Army hospital unit. The story portrays heroic American nurses working against fearful obstacles, providing feats of valor, and particularly emphasizing the dogged determination of the American troops, hospital staffs, and the Filipinos to resist the Japanese.

J079 Lansing, Elizabeth. *Nancy Naylor Flies South*. New York: Thomas Y. Crowell, 1943. 241p.

Here is one of several juvenile stories written especially for young girls. The heroine is Nancy Naylor who is by now an experienced airline hostess. The story begins in May of 1942 when she jumps at the opportunity to work on a new South American airline. The plot has her involved with Nazi spies, American diplomats, and various South American families.

The story verges on the improbable and the melodramatic. This is mundane juvenile stuff which now seems out of touch and out of date.

J080 Lattimore, Eleanor Frances. *Peachblossom*. New York: Harcourt, Brace, 1943. 96p.

Relates how a six-year-old Chinese orphan copes with the impact of the war in China. She is placed in a school where she is very much alone but is resolved to be cheerful. When an aunt is finally located who will take Peachblossom into her home, the little girl is genuinely happy in spite of the war and the loss of her immediate family. There is nothing of the actual horrors of war and battle. Rather, this is a child's view of the dislocations and evacuations forced upon her when her family is gone.

J081 Lent, Henry B[olles]. *Bombardier Tom Dixon Wins His Wings With the Bomber Command*. New York: Macmillan, 1943. 171p.

Describes the training of bombardiers starting with ground school and continuing with combat training at the Albuquerque Army Air Base, the Las Vegas Gunnery School, and mock target runs over a replica of the German industrial city of Essen laid out on the desert. By the end the bombardiers are headed for a secret Atlantic coastal base which is their dispersion site for combat duty assignments overseas.

J082 Lent, Henry B[olles]. *PT Boat: Bob Reed Wins His Command at Melville*. New York: Macmillan, 1943. 172p.

An account of the training a PT boat officer receives at the Motor Torpedo Boat center in Rhode Island. The story concludes with the exploits of several PT boats in the Bougainville area of the Pacific war.

J083 Maclean, Catherine Macdonald. *Three for Cordelia*. London: Collins, 1943. 192p. [Title in U.S.: *The Tharrus Three*. New York: Macmillan, 1943. 241p.]

This title continues the story about the children evacuated from the Glasgow slums to Cordelia's Scottish farm. Two of the young Scots and an ebullient Cockney boy are the principal characters. Although the war is a tangible element in the background, the main emphasis is on the life and activities of a highland farm and its relationship to the people of a nearby village. This is the sequel to *Seven for Cordelia* (item J22).

J084 Mason, Frank W. (pseud.) [Francis van Wyck Mason]. *Q-boat*. Philadelphia: Lippincott, 1943. 244p.

Two navy officers are the main protagonists in this story. William Dale and Rafe Holloway are assigned an old sailing brig and ordered to Ireland to rescue a blockaded convoy of merchant ships which have taken refuge in Breida Fjord to avoid destruction by the Germans. On the way, the brig is attacked and sunk by an enemy sub but the crew is rescued and brought safely home. Dale and Holloway are then given a new mission to locate the two German cruisers guarding another fjord entrance. They sink one with their only torpedo and manage to ram the other. And so on.

J085 Meader, Stephen Warren. *The Sea Snake*. New York: Harcourt, Brace, 1943. 255p.

An adventure tale placed on the coast of North Carolina during wartime. The sixteen-year-old son of a fisherman discovers a secret Nazi submarine base a short distance from his home. He is captured and taken aboard a German sub when he decides to observe their activities. He shrewdly plays the country bumpkin while soaking up all kinds of useful information about their espionage activities before he escapes. This story falls into the category of a slap-dash adventure tale for boys emphasizing aircraft, coast patrols, enemy subs, Nazi spies and the like.

J086 Montgomery, Rutherford George [Al Avery (pseud.)]. *Out of the Sun*. Philadelphia: David Mckay, 1943. 254p.

This is a Jack Armstrong type story for boys about four U.S. Marine fighter pilots in the early days of the Pacific war. The text is filled with heroics, hot-headed daring and the usual invincibility built into the heroes of juvenile formula fiction. Marty, Mel, O'Toole, and Ted leap from one fast-paced adventure or disaster to another, encompassing a commando raid on a Japanese base to commandeering Japanese bombers in order to escape. Naturally, they always succeed and everything turns out OK Jake!

J087 Montgomery, Rutherford George [Al Avery (pseud.)]. *War Wings*. Philadelphia: David Mckay, 1943. 224p.

Another title in this juvenile series featuring many of the same characters such as Stormy Marsh, a pilot in the RAF. The plot begins at an RAF base outside London with a night attack by the Germans. Blue Flight scrambles to meet the foe only to discover when they return to the field that one of the German planes is actually piloted by a Scotsman, McTavish, who has escaped from a German POW camp. He soon joins up with Stormy and Mel to be known as the three wolves. These three then go on to more daredevil exploits in the European air war and finally end up in the Pacific war against the Japanese. This is a typical juvenile war series filled with formula writing and a predictable Grub Street plot.

J088   Savery, Constance [Winifred]. *Enemy Brothers.* New York: Longmans, Green, 1943. 313p.

Max Eckerman, a twelve-year-old boy, has been abducted at an early age and brought up as the son of Nazi parents. The narrative covers his experiences when he is recognized in Norway as the long lost brother of an RAF pilot and taken back to England against his will. In spite of the resistance of Max who believes the English are all evil, his brother and his original parents, with extraordinary forebearance and understanding, win back the brainwashed and stubborn "little Hitler brother" to his original English heritage. The story points up the problem of re-educating Nazi children and also points out the divergent ideals of German children compared with those of English children. Max seems the most human of the characters. The other family members are cast as such paragons of virtue, friendliness and patience as to be too good to be true or real.

J089   Simmons, Margaret Irwin (pseud.) [Elisabeth Lansing]. *Sally Wins Her Wings.* New York: Thomas Y. Crowell, 1943. 258p.

A story for young girls which describes how a young American girl progresses from civilian pilot training to the RAF military ferry command in England during 1940 and 1941. An underlying theme is the deep-seated prejudice against women as pilots and the determined struggle of Sally Barnes to realize her ambition. The heroine is developed as a real person and a character of some depth.

J090   Snell, Roy Judson. *Norma Kent of the WACS.* Racine, WI: Whitman Publishing Company, 1943. 252p.

The heroine of this simple, melodramatic propaganda piece is Norma Kent, a recent college graduate. The WACS have just been recently formed. The story begins with her experiences in training (drill, K.P., study, inspections, etc.) at Fort Des Moines where she meets her service model, Lt. Rita Warren who convinces Norma to enter the Interceptor Control along the coastal areas of the U.S. They coordinate spotter reports on possible enemy sub and aircraft activities. The remainder of the story covers Norma's adventures with spies, mysterious U-boat landings, isolated observation huts, and the drama and romance of life for women in the WACS.

J091 Snell, Roy Judson. *Sally Scott of the WAVES*. Racine, WI: Whitman Publishing Company, 1943. 248p.

A story heavy on romance, mystery, propaganda and coincidence couched in a simplistic style. Sally and her friends in the U.S. Navy are traced through basic and advanced training and as they are assigned to regular duty with a convoy. Sally has a secret radio, a gift from a mysterious and eccentric inventor, which figures throughout Sally's adventures on land and on sea. Most of the action centers on a vital supply convoy to England and German sub attacks which Sally spots with her secret radio. Naturally, she saves the day (and the convoy) while her hero and boy friend Danny survives his crash-landing in the ocean. As one might expect there is a strong patriotic message throughout the narrative. Along with the Germans there is also a female villain in the WAVES whose jealousy of Sally and her friends leads to the sabotage of the ship's radio. Strictly for young and naive readers.

J092 Snell, Roy Judson. *Sparky Ames and Mary Mason of the Ferry Command*. Racine, WI: Whitman Publishing Company, 1943. 248p. [Title varies: *Sparky Ames of the Ferry Command*.]

The focus of this juvenile war story is the American Transport Air Command and many of its typical ferry missions throughout the world--from South America; to Africa, Persia and India, to China--and finally back to the U.S. The hero and heroine of the title are the dynamic male and female duo pilots who brave spies, sabotage attempts and the like to transport their top secret cargo from the U.S. via Brazil, etc. and eventually to China for use in the Allied bombing missions over Japan. The cargo is a new super bombsight. There is a hint of mystery and intrigue when Mary agrees to carry an ancient papyrus from Egypt back to an American Egyptologist who turns out to be a German spy in disguise. This is a standard "gee whiz" characterization that relies heavily on the juvenile series formula novels of the First World War.

J093   Stansbury, Jean. *Bars on Her Shoulders; A Story of a WAAC.* New York: Dodd, Mead, 1943. 276p.

This is the fictionalized treatment of the first class of women officer candidates commissioned in the Women's Army Auxiliary Corps (WAAC). The time period is that of the actual first class, July to September 1942 at Fort Des Moines. The heroine is Lacey Pendleton, a career girl who gives up her work to join the Army. The narrative takes her and her companions through the entire WAAC training, step by step. In effect, the text is really a recruitment device to acquaint and interest girls and young women in the Corps.

J094   Starret, William (pseud.) [Marshall McClintock]. *Nurse Blake Overseas.* New York: Gramercy Publishing Company, 1943. 256p.

Not seen.

J095   Waite, Jon. *Soldiers of the Sea.* New York: Cupples and Leon, 1943. 207p.

Here is a "gee whiz" adventure tale reminiscent of the typical juvenile serial literature of World War I. The wrapper has the subtitle: *A Story of the United States Marines.* Three Marine recruits, Red Monahan, Beef Grant, and Labs Burns join the Marines. Former college football jocks, they wax enthusiastic on sports and the traditions and training of the Marines. Their training and drill are covered as well as a suspected Nazi spy adventure in San Francisco before they ship out to Australia where they again encounter the same secret agent. Next, they assault a Japanese-held island, save their company from certain capture, and generally act and talk like twelve- and thirteen-year-olds who try to imagine what war is really like.

J096   Waite, Jon. *Wings Over Europe.* New York: Cupples and Leon, 1943. 208p.

A story about two Oklahoma ranch boys, Jim Patton and his friend Bill Sawdy. To become a pilot, Jim prepares for basic training at an army base. Bill becomes an airplane mechanic and is assigned with Jim throughout the war. In time Jim is sent to England, where they receive their bomber which they christen the *Oklahoma Girl*. In their first mission, Jim flies over northern France and bombs airfields at Caen and Paix. Later over Germany he is attacked by a German fighter and is forced to land somewhere in France. The five men in the *Oklahoma Girl* barely escape with their lives when the plane bursts into flames. After this they walk for nights until they reach the English Channel and find a boat that takes them back to England.

1944

J097 Avery, Al (pseud.) [Rutherford George Montgomery]. *A Yankee Flier in Italy*. New York: Grosset and Dunlap, 1944. 212p.

This is the fifth story in the Yankee Flier series. The three pilot chums, Lts. O'Malley, Wilson, and Allison, are now stationed in North Africa in preparation for the invasion of Sicily and Italy. O'Malley engenders the displeasure of the unit commander and is ordered to ferry fighter planes to Malta rather than air combat duty. His hot temperament and the devoted friendship of his buddies eventually result in a typical series of daredevil flying adventures, captures, and narrow escapes from the Germans. The story concludes with their rescue of Italian General Bolero in Italy and their escape flight to home base as the Germans begin the destruction of Naples. An action war story for boys based on a formula plot and character pattern characteristic of such juvenile series throughout the first half of the twentieth century.

J098 Avery, Al (pseud.) [Rutherford George Montgomery]. *A Yankee Flier Over Berlin*. New York: Grosset and Dunlap, 1944. 212p.

The sixth title in this series. The three pilot chums are finally split up. Allison has volunteered for bomber pilot duty over Germany while Wilson and O'Malley remain in the fighter escort wing. Wilson has his problems and crash-lands in the English Channel; then later in Germany where he and O'Malley are captured and sent to a prison camp. This leads to all sorts of spy activities such as Wilson's association with a Dutch quisling in the repair of a captured P-51 before his escape back to England. Another "gee whiz" formula war story for boys.

J099   Barne, Kitty. *Three and a Pigeon.* New York: Dodd, Mead, 1944. 206p.

This is a slight tale about daily life in an English country town during the war. The main character is Ivy, a young Cockney slum girl, who is bombed out of her London home. She is taken to the small town of Willowfield only to be bombed out again at the house of a doctor where she was boarded. The doctor and his family and Ivy pick up the pieces. The children meet a Belgian refugee boy who trains carrier pigeons. His employer is a chicken farmer who eventually is exposed as a black marketeer by the resourceful children. There seems ample mystery and humor in this low key adventure story for pre-adolescents. The question is whether the setting and the characters will especially appeal to contemporary children raised on heavy doses of television, particularly in the United States.

J100   Blackstock, Josephine. *Island on the Beam.* New York: Putnam, 1944. 221p.

A juvenile story about the struggle of Malta against the Axis forces as seen through the eyes of four children. Pietro, a twelve-year-old Maltese boy, is featured in his friendship with an English boy called John, his pilot brother, and an American friend. The action occurs before and during the hundred days of German bombardment. The narrative is well written and introduces much about the history of Malta and its people. The fighting closely affects the circumstances of the children. The book is an attempt to show the resolute unity of the Maltese to the threat of German invasion.

J101   Bowen, Robert Sidney. *Dave Dawson at Casablanca.* Akron: Saalfield, 1944. 250p.

Our two intrepid heroes of this series are now in the U.S. for a special intelligence mission to deliver six super secret letters to several countries in Latin America. A bizarre attack on their flight by a U-boat in the Caribbean is the beginning of a Nazi spy plot against the secret trip of President Roosevelt and his U.S. high command to Casablanca for a wartime conference with Churchill and his top brass. Sabotage attempts, and German air attacks on Freddy Farmer and Dave in their B-25 in mid-Atlantic all add up to an informant at the Allied headquarters in Casablanca. Once they land in North Africa, the two young heroes manage to infiltrate the secret air base of Goering's Snoopers in the Sahara. They make off with a

Messerschmitt and bomb all the Nazi planes at the base which, of course, prevents the German attack on Roosevelt's flight. Although wounded, the two make it back to Casablanca where they are immediately taken to the hospital. This is the thirteenth title in the author's War Adventure series.

J102   Bowen, Robert Sidney. *Dave Dawson With the Eighth Air Force*. Akron: Saalfield, 1944. 252p.

Not seen.

J103   Bowen, Robert Sidney. *Red Randall at Midway*. New York: Grosset and Dunlap, 1944. 210p.

The two intrepid heroes, Captain Red Randall and his flying mate, Captain Jimmy Joyce, are suddenly sent on a special and secret mission with eighteen other crack pilots on a Flying Fortress to New Caledonia to Funafuti to Kauai where they become aerial scouts to locate the position and number of ships in the Japanese Naval Task Force streaming towards Midway and other U.S. bases in the Pacific. In between stops they perform their usual daredevil exploits, destroy Zeros and the sub of the Jap fleet admiral that captured them after their crash-landing at sea. Then armed with strategic information from the sub they are rescued again by a Catalina Flying Boat only to be attacked by more Zeros. They manage to reach U.S. forces although wounded by the "Jap rats," and awake to find themselves in transit to the Hawaiian Islands where they will receive medals for their heroic actions.

J104   Bowen, Robert Sidney. *Red Randall at Pearl Harbor*. New York: Grosset and Dunlap, 1944. 216p.

The daring feats of Red and his buddy, Jimmy Joyce, have saved Hawaii from further Japanese attacks after Pearl Harbor. Early on December 7, 1941, on his way to a civilian airfield to put in flying practice, Red is assaulted by a Japanese agent. He reports the incident to American Intelligence, and is then requested to fly over the nearby bay from which an enemy submarine is expected to surface. Red watches as the sub explodes. Later he and his friend Jimmy are captured by the same Japanese agent and forced to fly the agent to a nearby island. But Red and Jimmy escape from the island and return to Oahu to see the havoc that has occurred in their absence. The important papers that Red has smuggled off the island tells American Intelligence of the future Japanese plans to attack the Hawaiian Islands. The first title of a series.

J105   Bowen, Robert Sidney. *Red Randall on Active Duty*. New York: Grosset and Dunlap, 1944. 211p.

Not seen.

J106   Bowen, Robert Sidney. *Red Randall on New Guinea*. New York: Grosset and Dunlap, 1944. 208p.

Not seen.

J107   Bowen, R[obert] Sidney. *Red Randall Over Tokyo*. New York: Grosset and Dunlap, 1944. 208p.

Recounts the experiences of two American fliers, Red Randall and his partner Jimmy Joyce in the South Pacific. Their mission is to infiltrate Japanese defenses on Honshu, make contact with intelligence agent No. 6, and return with urgently needed information. They find the agent near death, but he is able to pass on the vital data to the two heroes who return to Chungking via Tokyo on an aircraft carrier. Naturally, Red Randall and his sidekick never fail to accomplish their missions.

J108   Cook, Canfield. *Wings Over Japan*. New York: Grosset and Dunlap, 1944. 215p.

Squadron leader "Lucky" Robert Terrell and the Chinese military forces spend weeks of gruelling work to establish the Allied advance base in Chekiang Province with Stratohawk fighters escorting Lancaster bombers to their base in eastern China. These huge airplanes will fly across the Pacific to Japan. Guarded by the Stratohawk fighters, the bombers will pound Japanese naval bases, shipyards, industrial centers, and airfields. This important softening up of Japan is the prelude to the Allied invasion. Of course, Lucky is in the midst of this strategic enterprise.

J109   D'Aulaire, Ingri and Edgar Parin. *Wings for Per*. New York: Doubleday, Doran, 1944. 40p.

This is a picture book story using simple narrative technique to reach young children. The story describes young Per, his life along the steep coast of Norway, and how he escaped to Canada when the Germans invade. There he becomes a pilot at the Norwegian Air Force Training Center and eventually returns to Europe to help defeat the Nazis.

J110 Deming, Dorothy. *Penny and Pam, Nurse and Cadet*. New York: Dodd, Mead, 1944. 230p.

Penelope "Penny" Marsh Bridgeman, R.N., is a Red Cross nurse assigned to investigate nursing possibilities during and after the war. Penny's uncle has asked her to permit his niece, Pamela, to accompany her. As the trip progresses, Pamela discovers that nursing is the occupation which she wishes to follow, and decides which school she should attend. The novel depicts wartime nursing, recruiting, and the opportunities presented for nurses during and after the war. A didactic tale for older girls.

J111 Downey, Fairfax Davis. *Jezebel the Jeep*. New York: Dodd, Mead, 1944. 150p.

A light-hearted war story probably for boys about the adventures of a jeep. A young soldier called Johnny is the driver. He names the jeep *Jezebel* when his girl writes him a dear John letter. Johnny then becomes the driver for a captain in a series of adventures concluding in Sicily where the jeep is smashed to bits during an attack by the Germans and Johnny is seriously wounded and sent back to the states to recuperate.

J112 Duncan, Gregory (pseud.) [Marshall McClintock]. *Dick Donnelly of the Paratroops*. Racine, WI: Whitman, 1944. 248p.

The fifth title in his Fighters for Freedom series. Not seen.

J113 Duncan, Gregory (pseud.) [Marshall McClintock]. *March Anson and Scoot Bailey of the U.S. Navy*. Racine, WI: Whitman, 1944. 248p.

The seventh title in his Fighters for Freedom series. Not seen.

J114 Embury, Lucy. *Pan Paderewski's Easter*. New Canaan: Privately printed, 1944. 44p.

This appears to be a juvenile fable placed during and after the liberation of Poland. The text is filled with Polish folk images in almost a rhapsodic fantasy combining wildlife (hares, foxes, wolves, etc.), the forest, and patriotic symbols from Polish history. Two small boys, Anhelli and his older brother Jannz, are representative of the half-starved and wild children of wartime Poland. They find refuge inside a large oak tree and live off the land. Jannz is killed by a bomb and Anhelli is left completely alone until he accidentally runs into Mary whom he confuses with Panna Marya (Christ's mother). In a sense, she rescues the boy from the wilds and promises him love and peace in Warsaw at the new Paderewski Home for Children.

J115   Felsen, [Henry] Gregor. *Some Follow the Sea.* New York: Dutton, 1944. 192p.

The narrative describes Chris Hollister, a seventeen-year-old boy who, rejected by the navy, is determined to serve his country. He enters the Merchant Marine and ships out on an old freighter carrying horses bound for England. The ship is torpedoed and the loss of the animals provides a dramatic and emotional aspect to these lend/lease voyages during the war. Chris and his Scottish friend live through many harrowing experiences of air and submarine attacks; are more than once forced to abandon ship as they crew to Murmansk and back. Chris is described as an average youngster with no actual training for battle at sea. This is a matter-of-fact view of life on a wartime merchant vessel with realistic descriptions of the conditions and problems of the crews. Over thirty actual photographs of life at sea on these ships are included in order to lend authenticity to the fictional narrative, although the wartime propaganda purpose seems obvious.

J116   Gleit, Maria   (pseud.) [Hertha Gleitsmann]. *Pierre Keeps Watch.* New York: Scribner, 1944. 211p.

Set in France during the early war years, the hero is a thirteen-year-old shepherd boy who lives in a small mountain village. When the Germans eventually arrive to appropriate their animals, Perre manage to save the village herds of sheep and goats from the hands of the Germans. The narrative portrays the wartime life and the strong and abiding patriotism of the French villagers. Pierre has many hair-raising adventures but he and his Resistance friends are only able to rest easy when the German troops are finally withdrawn for the Italian front. There is little wartime violence in this largely pastoral testiment to French steadfastness and character. Considering the date of publication and the story, there is an obvious propaganda element, understandable as it may be.

J117   Gronowicz, Antoni. *Four From the Old Town.* Translated from the Polish by Joseph Vetter. New York: Scribner, 1944. 149p.

A juvenile story about four Polish teenagers in Lwow, Poland. One of the boys discovers that a teacher at his high school is a secret Nazi sympathizer. Shortly thereafter the Germans invade Poland, bombing cities and villages before occupying Lwow. One of the four is killed when he tries to avenge his family. The others join the resistance to help free the city from German domination. This is a relatively brief account of the Nazi occupation covering the usual incidents-- Jewish harassments and the like.

J118   Harkins, Philip. *Bomber Pilot*. New York: Harcourt, 1944. 229p.

A juvenile story that traces the training and combat experiences of Lt. Al Hudson and his comrades in the European war. The descriptions of training camp and combat flight preparation are extremely detailed and probably as authentic as a juvenile could wish. The story begins with training in Tennessee and England and concludes with combat missions over Germany in a Flying Fortress bomber. The characterization tends to be single-dimensional and sketchy.

J119   Johns, Williams Earl. *Biggles in the Orient*. London: Hodder and Stoughton, 1944. 179p.

Describes the Japanese attempt to disrupt the air supply route from Burma to China and how Biggles foils their efforts. Not seen.

J120   Johns, William Earl. *Gimlet Goes Again: King of the Commandos in an Exciting Adventure with Fighting France and the Grey Fleas of the North*. Bickley: University of London Press, 1944. 185p.

This author has maintained the tradition of the boys' series stories so prevalent during and after the First World War and largely gone by World War II. Here is a war adventure tale with all of the typical action, suspense, and super exploits characteristic of Tom Swift and all the other fictional boy heroes. Thus, the plot is formula and insignificant except to say the boys of the story conceal their real names by adopting those of wild forest animals--Louis is the Fox; Nigel is the Cub; the others are the Hawk, Grasshopper, Snake, etc. in an underground organization operating in Nazi-occupied France which the boys call "The Grey Fleas of the North." Cub is taken back to England with some British commandos and reveals the activities of the "Grey Fleas." Cub Peters now

serves as the liaison between Captain Gimlet King and his men
"Copper" and "Trapper" and the boy saboteurs in France as
they engage the Germans in one adventure after another.

J121   Johns, William Earl. *Worrals Goes East*. London: Hodder and
        Stoughton, 1944. 192p.

        She heads to India with the WAAF. Not seen.

J122   Johnson, Martha (pseud.) [Elizabeth Carleton Lansing]. *Sandra
        Mitchell Stands By*. New York: Thomas Y. Crowell, 1944.
        192p.

        Here is a very traditional juvenile story for girls. The plot
        begins in New York City where Sandra's father is a prominent
        doctor. She is given the Glamor Girl of 1943 award but is
        basically a spoiled young woman who has no serious purpose
        or interest in life, even joining the WAC or WAVES military
        groups to serve her country. But when her father has a heart
        attack and moves to his home town to practice medicine again,
        she becomes involved in a number of mysterious local
        happenings, a fire and a train wreck, and is instrumental in the
        apprehension of a spy for the Nazis, who has attempted a
        number of sabotage efforts in the region. She, of course, is
        destined also for a new romance with a young man who in the
        end turns out to be the undercover FBI agent in the local
        investigation of the suspected spy. Sandra by now has matured
        and accepted responsibility and becomes the didactic example
        that the juvenile female reader requires, or was thought to back
        in the 1940s.

J123   Lansing, Elizabeth. *Nancy Naylor, Flight Nurse*. New York:
        Thomas Y. Crowell, 1944. 167p.

        This is a wartime juvenile adventure featuring an airline
        stewardess who decides to do her part for the war effort by
        training as a flight nurse. The narrative follows her through the
        rigors and excitement of the African, Sicilian, and Italian
        battlefronts as she helps in flying the Allied wounded to
        hospitals. There is the expected element of low-key romance to
        add a love interest for older girls.

J124   Lent, Henry B[olles]. *Seabee: Bill Scott Builds and Fights for
        the Navy*. New York: Macmillan, 1944. 176p.

        A detailed description of the U.S. Navy's Construction
        Battalions, or "Seabees." The Seabee official motto is "We

build--we fight" but the Seabees have changed it to "Can do, will do--Did!" and they consider their official uniform soggy boots, dungarees, and a rain hat. Bill Scott and his comrades are trained at Camp Endicott in Rhode Island. Their arrival at "Island X" and the way in which a newly captured island is readied for the arrival of American troops is described in detail.

J125 Maclean, Catherine Macdonald. *Farewell to Tharrus*. New York: Macmillan, 1944. 205p.; London: Collins, 1944. 160p.

This story completes the author's trilogy about the children evacuated from the city slums to Tharrus, a wooded farm in the Scottish Highlands. The final title sums up the impact of the war on the community, and acknowledges the blessings which the war cannot touch such as the beauty of nature and the humanity of mankind. One of the major changes in this community involves some overseas soldiers stationed in the neighborhood, and their relationships with the children and the people of the area. Like all the other Tharrus novels, this last installment, though sentimental, is still a testament to the kindness and dignity of the Scottish people. The previous titles of the trilogy are *Seven for Cordelia* (1941) and *The Tharrus Three* (1943).

J126 Mason, Frank W. (pseud.) [Francis van Wyck Mason]. *Pilots, Man Your Planes!* Philadelphia: Lippincott, 1944. 213p.

The action takes place in the Pacific and in the Mediterranean war theaters. The hero is Captain Hugh Steel who must battle not only the Japanese but also the jealous incompetence of his know-it-all commander. Of course, Steel wins out, is promoted and transferred to help in the defense of the Mediterranean area where he continues his heroic and action-filled activities, e.g., bombing the Brenner Pass and blocking Nazi plans to bomb Malta. A fictionalized attempt to glorify the men of the U.S. Army Air Force.

J127 Montgomery, Rutherford [George]. *Warhawk Patrol*. Philadelphia: David Mckay, 1944. 246p.

Recounts the experiences of pilot Lieutenant Marty Rivers, and Sergeant Hash Hinkle, an airplane mechanic, in north Africa as they find themselves in the midst of a Nazi plot to capture and destroy their airplane. Recognizing a Nazi infiltrator, the two men follow him, only to be captured themselves. When they manage to escape by commandeering one of the Nazis' planes, they fly to their headquarters with vital enemy information.

J128 Norton, Andre (pseud.) [Alice Mary Norton]. *The Sword is Drawn*. Boston: Houghton Mifflin, 1944. 178p.

The hero of this story is eighteen-year-old Lorens Van Norreys, the heir to an ancient firm of jewel merchants in Holland. The action begins in June of 1942 when the head of the house of Norreys summons his grandson to his bedside to give him instructions about the distribution of the business under the Nazi occupation. Lorens escapes to England after leaving in a secret safe the Flowers of Orange--a priceless family necklace--that can be opened only after two years and by a special word! The young man fights in Java, escapes to Australia, then to the United States and England before eventually making his way back to Rotterdam to regain the famous necklace and use it to help finance the Netherlands Royal Air Force stationed in England.

J129 Procter, Leslie C[hambers]. *For Freedom's Sake*. Chicago: Beckley-Cardy, 1944. 347p.

A combination travelogue and history lesson about Washington, D.C. and its environs during the war. Uncle Ted Wilson, an FBI agent, escorts his niece and nephew on a two-week visit to the city. During this time Uncle Ted describes the places involved in the war in order to teach patriotism to the two young children. They learn about Hitler, Himmler, German militarism, and the meaning of the Gestapo and Nazism. Other discussions cover the meaning of quisling, what happened at Dunkirk, and how the Japanese attacked Pearl Harbor.

J130 Radford, Ruby Lorraine. *Kitty Carter, Canteen Girl*. Racine, WI: Whitman Publishing Company, 1944. 248p.

A war story for girls which is clearly designed to create a sense of service for the war effort. Kitty dreams of joining the WAVES but is forced to remain at home to care for her younger brother who has no one else. Kitty finds that she can still be a Canteen girl and do her part. She lives with her father who is in the naval medical corps at a military hospital by a Marine base in the southern U.S. Kitty soon senses an intrigue at the hospital, undertakes a boat trip to an island in the marshes on the coast and discovers a secret German U-boat supply depot. This, of course, leads to spies and all sorts of excitement. The basic message is that one can serve even at home. Otherwise, this is typical and stereotypical fare for adolescents.

J131 Radford, Ruby Lorraine. *Nancy Dale, Army Nurse*. Racine, WI: Whitman Publishing Company, 1944. 248p.

Relates the experiences of Nancy Dale who, upon graduation from nursing school, enlists in the Army Nursing Corps. The story follows Nancy's career through army basic training, and then when she is posted overseas to northern Australia. Here Nancy is reunited with her brother Tom, a United States air pilot, who was rescued on a South Pacific island, after having been shot down by the Japanese.

J132 Riesenberg, Felix. *Phantom Freighter*. New York: Dodd, Mead, 1944. 180p.

A wartime espionage story that takes place in the summer of 1943 on a freighter headed to a South Sea island. The white-painted and unarmed vessel is on a confidential mission which is never disclosed. In spite of traitors on board and submarine attacks, the freighter completes her mission (whatever it is) and returns bringing captives and counter-espionage information.

J133 Roberts, Terence. *Mystery Schooner*. New York: Viking Press, 1944. 271p.

A group of five young people--American, Dutch, Chinese, and Malayan--escape from the Japanese when they invade Sumatra. The five accidentally find an abandoned but completely equipped schooner which they sail all the way to South Africa. Their adventures include an attack by both a Japanese aircraft and destroyer, a German sub, typhoon, and a shipwreck. The alternate danger and extreme boredom have their effect on the young crew of eighteen-year-olds. The various improbabilities are not overcome by the attempt of the author to create an atmosphere of reality throughout this juvenile mystery.

J134 Seymour, Alta Halverson. *On the Edge of the Fjord*. Philadelphia: Westminster Press, 1944. 212p.

Describes the patriotic resistance and adventures of fourteen-year-old Petra Engeland, her brother Martin, and their friend Peter and others when the Germans occupy their fishing village in Norway. There is much about hiding in local caves, escapes up mountain trails and in fishing skiffs, etc. in order to foil the enemy soldiers and their collaborators.

J135   Shurtleff, Bertrand Leslie. *AWOL K-9 Commando.* Indianapolis: Bobbs-Merrill, 1944. 284p.

This juvenile tale introduces AWOL, a Doberman Pinscher war dog who has been trained and abused by his German military masters. He is taken from them by an American working in Germany shortly before Pearl Harbor. Before the U.S. enters the war, the American, George Stanhope, returns to the U.S., enlists in the Army Air Force, and sends the Doberman to the Dogs for Defense program for training. Both are returned separately to England where AWOL is assigned two trainers with whom the dog performs liaison duties by carrying messages between raiding parties and the command post until enemy fire separates AWOL from his handlers. In a series of fortuitous incidents, the dog is reunited with Stanhope who is now a German war prisoner. After a daring escape, the two are sent back to the U.S. for treatment of their war wounds.

J136   Snell, Roy Judson. *Jet Plane Mystery.* Chicago: Wilcox and Follet, 1944. 244p.

Ensign Jack Steel and his pilot buddies Stew, Ted, Kentucky, etc. are on the carrier *Black Bee* in the mid-Pacific to fight the Japs. Jack is a scout pilot sent out to report on the activities of the enemy. But he and his buddy Stew are shot down in the ocean near an island that they are able to reach. There Jack discovers the presence of a jet plane. He also discovers a native tribe whose slim girl turns out to be Mary Brown, a nurse from the States! Suffice it to say that Jack also carries his violin with him in his airplane and has taken it to the island where he serenades the tribe members. Anyhow, while Jack fiddles, his pilot buddies continue the air war against the Jappies. Then Jack, fascinated by the island presence of the jet plane, takes an opportunity to steal it and fly it back to the carrier where it becomes a fabulous scout and fighter plane. This is authentic juvenile "gee whiz" war adventure fiction of the 1940s and 1950s. It is difficult to see how the current generation would read or even care about this old-fashioned material.

J137   Sowers, Phyllis. *Swords and Sails in the Philippines.* Chicago: Whitman, 1944. 127p.

A war adventure tale which describes the experiences of a young Moro boy in the Philippines when the Japanese invade. Abdul is a thirteen-year-old on the island of Mindanao who is the hero and central character. There is an effort to show the patriotic courage of the natives and their strong desire for independence. Interspersed with this are plenty of details on island customs and the nature of life in the tropics. When Abdul meets an American officer, he soon becomes instrumental in encouraging Moro support for the U.S. forces. Nonetheless, the story is contrived and unconvincing.

J138 Starret, William (pseud.) [Marshall McClintock]. *Nurse Blake at the Front*. New York: Gramercy Publishing Company, 1944. 253p.

Not seen.

J139 Stieff, Frederick Philip. *Unleash the Dogs of War, A Story*. New York: Robert M. McBride, 1944. 227p.

This is the story of Cecil of the K-9 corps, as told by one of Cecil's masters, Murky, who was recruited after he enlisted in the military. Murky describes the K-9 training at Front Royal, Virginia, and Cecil's contribution in the North African campaign, his return to the United States after being wounded, and his reunion with his master, who also had been wounded.

J140 Wells, Helen [Frances]. *Cherry Ames, Army Nurse*. New York: Grosset and Dunlap, 1944. 214p.

After graduation with her class from Spencer Hospital, Cherry joins the Armed Forces as an Army nurse with the rank of lieutenant. Sent through basic training which involved camping out in tents, digging foxholes and slit trenches, and considerable marching, she is assigned to hospital duty in Panama. There she is instrumental in furthering research for a malaria cure. The inspirational element does not make up for the absence of literary style or accomplished writing ability.

J141 Wells, Helen [Frances]. *Cherry Ames, Chief Nurse*. New York: Grosset and Dunlap, 1944. 213p.

Covers the further adventures of Cherry on a South Pacific island with American Army troops. She serves as the chief nurse of their field hospital. In the jungle, tents and barracks become a hospital for the injured troops as they are brought from the battlefield. All of the nurses try to make these quarters as livable and homelike as possible for the troops and themselves. Cherry is even able to meet up with her twin brother who just happens to fly in as a member of the Air Transport Command.

J142   Wells, Helen [Frances]. *Cherry Ames, Senior Nurse*. New York: Grosset and Dunlap, 1944. 217p.

Cherry describes her training as a nurse in the final years of the war. Although the conflict is coming to a close, many nurses are still needed. The narrative provides a view of all the exciting developments in the world of medicine and the varied facets of the medical units as well as emphasizing the continued need for research that produces such products as penicillin. Senior Nurse Ames is delighted that all of her graduating class decide to volunteer for service as Army nurses. This is a typical didactic propaganda piece devised to encourage interest in Army nursing and service.

1945

J143   Avery, Al (pseud.) [Rutherford George Montgomery]. *A Yankee Flier in Normandy*. New York: Grosset and Dunlap, 1945. 209p.

The three daredevil RAF pilots are now sent to an English estate where they are to be assigned to secret pre-invasion missions into German-occupied France. Stan Wilson is transferred to a desk job to plan part of the D-Day operation through a series of supply drops to the French underground. O'Malley is shot down and Wilson joins with Allison to complete the French maquis mission. They also crash-land, discover O'Malley, and soon escape back to England in a decrepit antique aeroplane. They then join an air troop parachute drop behind the Nazi lines and capture a strategic bridge that will help the Normandy landings. Amidst the usual heroic and daring exploits, the three heroes wind up the seventh war adventure in this juvenile series.

J144   Avery, Al (pseud.) [Rutherford George Montgomery]. *A Yankee Flier on a Rescue Mission*. New York: Grosset and Dunlap, 1945. 210p.

O'Malley, Allison, and Wilson continue their fearless adventures as pilots in the air war against the Germans in Europe. They are now flying fighter escort for Allied bombers over Europe and Berlin. Most of the action deals with the efforts of Wilson and O'Malley to locate Allison after he is shot down over Germany. When he is spotted in a prison camp the two chums hatch a plot to rescue him using a captured German aircraft in a false crash-landing. All three end up together as prisoners but a clever ruse and the usual improbable incidents and behavior enable the friends to escape, steal an enemy officer's car, then a plane, and reach Allied lines safely. This is another improbable juvenile tale of heroic war exploits that bears little resemblance to the reality of war. This is the eighth title in the series.

J145 Barne, Kitty [Marion Catherine Streatfield]. *In the Same Boat*. London: Dent, 1945. 218p.; New York: Dodd, Mead, 1945. 208p.

Describes Bridget, an English girl, and Antosia, a young spirited Polish refugee, who meet aboard a ship taking them from India to England. After the vessel is torpedoed and they are rescued from lifeboats, they reach the English home of Bridget's grandmother. The girls then are enrolled in the school which Bridget's mother and grandmother both attended. Antosia acquaints her new school mates on Poland's position in the war. Suddenly Antosia's father who is in the Polish underground, escapes from Poland and suddenly appears at the school. As the story concludes, the father returns again to Poland to aid the resistance against the Nazis.

J146 Bowen, Robert Sidney. *Dave Dawson on the Russian Front*. Akron: Saalfield, 1945. 252p.

The two heroes are now back in England where they receive their new assignment from Colonel Welsh and the RAF Vice-Marshal for Intelligence. Over three years ago a special Allied agent had been arrested in Poland by the Germans just as he was set to contact a man called Nikolsk for the last piece of strategic intelligence information. The boys are now to serve as decoys for the Gestapo so that an agent can slip secretly into Russia and behind German lines to Tobolsk and contact Nikolsk, if he is still alive. Naturally, Dave and Freddy and the agent all manage to evade, escape, and daringly carry out their mission in this tenth story in the War Adventure series.

J147 Bowen, Robert Sidney. *Red Randall in Burma*. New York: Grosset and Dunlap, 1945. 210p.

Red and his friend Jimmy are now assigned to the U.S. Twelfth Army Air Force in the India-Burma-China war theater. The boys are en route to Calcutta aboard a troop transport. Torpedoed by a Japanese sub, the boys are rescued and taken captive by the sub. When the sub is later depth-bombed, Red and Jimmy manage to escape when the vessel is forced to surface, and are picked up by a British ship. The boys then join the RAF in a plan to rescue a group of British soldiers surrounded by Japanese troops in the Burmese jungle. Their hazardous mission is, of course, successful and they fight off the enemy attacks. This is the seventh title in this series.

J148   Bowen, Robert Sidney. *Red Randall in the Aleutians*. New York: Grosset and Dunlap, 1945. 214p.

Describes the experiences of Navy pilots Red Randall and his friend, Jimmy Joyce, just before the American invasions against the Japanese in Attu and Kiska in the Aleutians. Red and his chums spot an enemy cruiser their first time out and later discover a Japanese baby flat-top with destroyer escort. The daring duo are successful in avoiding enemy Zeros, and score four hits on one of the vessels. A typical rah, rah boys' war story.

J149   Cook, Canfield. *The Flying Jet*. New York: Grosset and Dunlap, 1945. 210p.

Covers the adventures of RAF Wing Commander "Lucky" Robert Terrell, as he becomes involved in fighting Nazi rockets with the latest type of secret British aircraft, the Stratojet, the fastest plane in the world. After he is ordered to report at once to the British Embassy in Washington, D.C., he learns he is to fly Senor X, a rocket expert, into Germany in order to discover the exact location of the Nazi rocket research program.

J150   Dean, Graham M. *Wings Over the Desert*. New York: Viking Press, 1945. 224p.

Features a young Nevada reporter, Andy Hughes, who joins the Civil Air Patrol after Pearl Harbor. The plot has Japanese saboteurs and dramatic air operations over the Nevada desert by CAP personnel.

J151   Ford, Edward. *Larry Scott of the Sun*. Philadelphia: Macrae-Smith, 1945. 251p.

Traces the early career of journalist Larry Scott, after he leaves high school to cover local stories for his town newspaper. He is then noticed and hired by a Philadelphia International Press Bureau. This occurs at the same time Hitler launches his blitzkrieg against the Low Countries. Larry is now sent to Burma to cover the war there, and arrives in the Philippines just in time to be caught in the battle for Manila. He accompanies the troops to Bataan and to Corregidor, and afterwards leaves for Australia and hence home to the States.

J152   Gibbs, Philip Hamilton. *Through the Storm*. London: Hutchinson, 1945. 320p.

Describes how the lives of the three Hambledon children from New England are altered by the war years between Pearl Harbor and D-Day. Edward who lived an artist's life in Paris before the fall of France, joins the maquis. Tiny, the pacifist brother, joins the American Army after Pearl Harbor. The sister, who is in love with a British naval officer, joins the Red Cross. The three characters are stereotypes while the plot is a familiar formula approach.

J153   Gleit, Maria (pseud.) [Hertha Gleitsmann]. *Katrina*. New York: Scribner, 1945. 239p.

The time ranges from 1942 to November 1944 in German occupied Luxembourg. Katrina, a young girl, is invited to live with her uncle and aunt. After she walks the fifteen miles to their home, she soon is involved in assisting an old pastor to organize a prohibited pilgrimage to the religious shrine of Our Lady. In the process she beomes involved with the Resistance and finds herself in one exciting adventure after another. There are brushes with Nazi troops, mob scenes, and a general atmosphere of how uncertain life can be under an occupied army for such a long time. The narrative is also a testimonial to the probity of the people of Luxembourg.

J154   Hazlett, Edward Everett. *"Rig For Depth Charges!" The Career of a Young Naval Officer on Submarine Duty*. New York: Dodd, Mead, 1945. 269p.

Relates the experiences of Robert "Saint" Rodney, a sub officer on convoy duty in the Atlantic and on patrol duty in the South Pacific. The action begins in Honolulu on December 7, 1941, as the Saint's ship is sunk. A German espionage agent who serves as a signaler for the Japanese Navy reappears from time to time. After the loss of his ship, Rodney is sent to submarine school in Connecticut, and afterwards assigned to a sub that sees action in both the Atlantic and the Pacific oceans. Although the author has thirty years of active duty in the navy, this does not for good fiction make.

J155   Johns, Williams Earl. *Worrals of the Islands; A Story of the War in the Pacific*. London: Hodder and Stoughton, 1945. 192p.

Covers the activities of Worals and her WAAF friends in the Pacific war. Not seen.

J156   Johnson, Martha (pseud.) [Elisabeth Carleton Lansing]. *Ann Bartlett Returns to the Philippines*. New York: Thomas Y. Crowell, 1945. 216p.

Another title in this juvenile series for prepubescent girls that lauds the experiences and contributions of nurses in the Pacific war. The story begins in San Francisco when Ann is assigned to the Sea Haven hospital ship on a new tour of duty that will go from Hawaii and Guam to the Philippines. The plot describes the heroic efforts of Ann and her male support crew when they are separated from their hospital ship. Their life boat is strafed by the Japanese and sunk as they attempt to rescue the men on a damaged destroyer. The bulk of the action covers their beaching and jungle survival trek to avoid capture by the Japanese forces. The action concludes with Ann and her friends viewing the U.S. invasion fleet in the Lingayen Gulf and Ann re-united with her hospital ship.

J157   Lent, Henry Bolles. *Ahoy, Shipmate! Steve Ellis Joins the Merchant Marine*. New York: Macmillan, 1945. 192p.

Much of the information that is used to praise the protagonist, Steve Ellis, is based on the U.S. Maritime Service. The narrative describes the training given to the men in the merchant marine. Steve learns quickly, makes high grades to earn an O.S. (Ordinary Seaman) rank. After boot camp Steve is ordered to his duty ship which leaves in a convoy headed for the Firth of Clyde. From Scotland the boat goes to Murmansk but is attacked by German aircraft en route. When Steve returns to a safe port in the United States, he is cited for gallant action. This is a formula juvenile story with an especially heavy dose of patriotic propaganda to inspire young readers back then.

J158   MacKaye, David Loring. *The Twenty-fifth Mission*. New York, Toronto: Longmans, Green, 1945. 214p.

Jigs, the protagonist in this juvenile war story is a seventeen-year-old tail gunner on an American bomber. On their twenty-fifth mission several of the crew are killed and the survivors are forced to bail out over occupied Denmark. They are rescued by the underground and eventually smuggled to Copenhagen, then into Sweden. Jigs in the process grows up, mans a machine gun in Copenhagen, loses his provincial suspicion of foreigners, and discovers what he is really fighting for in the war.

J159   Means, Florence Crannell. *The Moved Outers*. Boston: Houghton Mifflin, 1945. 154p.

Based on the incarceration of the Japanese-Americans in special camps in the western United States, the action begins with the attack on Pearl Harbor and describes the experiences of the Ohara family starting with the arrest of the father by the FBI and the placement of the entire family in a Relocation camp. The protagonists are Sue and Kim Ohara, both in their teens. Based on fact, the story explains the treatment and the general attitudes of and toward Japanese-Americans in the United States during the early war years.

J160   Montgomery, Rutherford George. *Thunderboats, Ho!* Philadelphia: David Mckay, 1945. 256p.

The Guadalcanal beachhead and other islands are the background for the breaking up of the "Tokyo Express." The plot describes the daring exploits of Lieutenant Mike Moran with a small task force of U.S. PT boats in the South Pacific. They carry out their mission to sink a Japanese aircraft-carrier and safely return to base. The men are augmented by a wily and trustworthy native called Malop who has a grudge of his own to settle with the Japanese.

J161   Neumann, Daisy. *Now That April's There*. Chicago: Consolidated Book Publishers, 1945. 224p.; Philadelphia: Lippincott, 1945. 224p.

Fifteen-year-old Wincy Turner has spent three years in Cambridge, Massachusetts as an English evacuee. She now returns to England where her father is a don at Oxford University. She has become a young lady, much to the bewilderment of her parents, who persist in still treating her as a child. She in turn is confused by the contrasts between American and English life and customs. The presence of American and British soldiers, rationing, and other inconveniences of wartime, nevertheless serve to remind her of the war.

J162   Riesenberg, Felix. *Man on a Raft*. New York: Dodd, Mead, 1945. 192p.

A juvenile spy mystery placed aboard a liberty ship in the Pacific war zone. The vessel leaves from San Pedro on sealed orders with an assorted crew that soon creates disciplinary problems for the first mate and the captain. One of the crew turns out to be a spy for the enemy. After the usual submarine threat, the ship reaches Guadalcanal and its rendezvous to pick up marines to be sent home. In reality this is all a cover for the removal of a group of spy prisoners from the island to facilities elsewhere.

J163   Shurtleff, Bertrand Leslie. *Short Leash*. Indianapolis: Bobbs-Merrill, 1945. 270p.

When two British officers are shot down in the mountains of New Guinea, a search force from the United States K-9 Corps is sent to locate them. The team consists of Lieutenant Sedgewick, Sergeant Trueman, and two dogs, Spareribs and Huskie. The team finds itself almost immediately in impenetrable jungles which are inhabited by deeply-entrenched Japanese troops at a secret base, as well as native cannibals. Nevertheless, the team finds the two officers and rescues them from the natives who had captured them. Unable to travel because of their weakened condition and malaria, the team sends their dog Spareribs back to their base at Port Moresby, with a message for help and a warning about the secret Japanese base. The dog arrives after a hazardous trek and a plane is sent to rescue the men while parachute troops attack the Japanese base and overrun the enemy.

J164   Simmons, Margaret Irwin (pseud.) [Elisabeth Lansing]. *Kay Allen on Overseas Mission*. New York: Thomas Y. Crowell, 1945. 256p.

An espionage story for teenage girls featuring an American girl who is sent by the federal government to obtain vital information from a friend held as a German prisoner in Belgrade. Although there is plenty of suspense, intrigue and mystery, it is all based on a most improbable plot. The strong and resolute purpose of the Yugoslav partisans is the more convincing aspect of this dated tale for girls.

J165 Sperry, Armstrong. *Hull-down For Action*. Garden City, N.Y.: Doubleday, 1945. 213p.

This is a South Pacific adventure story that is set in the early months of the Pacific war. Jeff Anders, skipper of a pearling boat, is set adrift on a raft on December 7 of 1941 with three of his crew by the Japanese steward and an enemy spy on the crew. The four on the raft drift south and eventually reach Guadalcanal. Here they are afflicted with problems in the jungle such as disease and their inability to communicate with the pygmies and native tribes. Shortly they spot their old pearling boat in a nearby bay drifting to shore. They board the vessel and sail it to Australia where they all enlist in the U.S. Marines!

J166 Van der Haas, Henrietta. *Orange on Top*. New York: Harcourt, Brace, 1945. 221p.

A story for young juveniles about the German occupation of Holland. The narrow focus of the plot is upon three intrepid Dutch children and their courageous efforts to protect and to save a small Jewish girl from the Nazi roundup of Jews. The larger emphasis is upon the general Dutch resistance to the Nazi rule. There is an obvious propaganda aspect to the story.

J167 Wells, Helen [Frances]. *Cherry Ames, Flight Nurse*. New York: Grosset and Dunlap, 1945. 215p.

Cherry now becomes a "flying angel" in a medical air evacuation unit. Posted to England, her new assignment is to fly with the wounded soldiers from the bomber base in England to the hospital in Prestwick, Scotland. She also flies beyond enemy lines to pick up the wounded and care for them on their return trip to England.

1946

J168 Berger, Josef. *Counterspy Jim*. Boston: Little, Brown, 1946. 308p.

Here is a juvenile spy adventure featuring naval lieutenant Jim Ellis. Jim is assigned to undercover spy duty on a freighter which appears to be the source of messages sent to enemy U-

boats. He is disguised as a messman. In the course of his
mission everything happens that could be anticipated in the
Battle of the Atlantic. He is torpedoed more than once and
drifts for days in a lifeboat. He is picked up by a German U-
boat filled with saboteurs headed for Cape Cod and
experiences depth bomb attacks by the Allies. Naturally, he
successfully completes his mission. The text contains a
substantial amount of naval technical details with good
characterization and writing.

J169   Bowen, Robert Sidney. *Dave Dawson at Truk*. Akron:
        Saalfield, 1946. 243p.; New York: Crown, 1946. 243p.

        Freddy and Dave are at the San Diego Naval Air Base to
help train Army and Navy pilots. They accidentally overhear a
Japanese spy and a traitorous U.S. Naval officer conferring on
how the traitor will sabotage a carrier task force in the Pacific.
After the two heroes are attacked and wounded, they fly on to
Pearl Harbor to help identify the pilot on one of the aircraft
carriers. On the way their bomber is sabotaged but they safely
arrive only to be abducted and imprisoned outside Honolulu by
Japanese spies. By a clever ruse they manage to be freed but
too late to stop the task force departure. They again are sent off
by air to reach the carrier task force. They finally spot the
traitor just before the mission take-off and both Dave and
Freddy follow him towards Truk. When Dave's guns jam he
crashes his plane into the traitor's, nearly losing his life in the
process. Although seriously wounded, Dave parachutes to the
ocean and with the help of his buddy survives to learn of the
destruction of the Japs at Truk by their carrier task force. This
is the fifteenth story in the War Adventure series for juveniles.

J170   Bowen, Robert Sidney. *Dave Dawson Over Berlin*. Akron:
        Saalfield, 1946. 203p.

        Not seen.

J171   Bowen, R[obert] Sidney. *Red Randall's One-Man War*. New
        York: Grosset and Dunlap, 1946. 215p.

        Three years after the Bataan Death March and the
occupation of the Philippines by Japanese forces, Air Force
Captains Red Randall and Jimmy Joyce are sent on a mission to
Luzon. They are to contact a guerrilla force led by American
Navy Lieutenant Jackson in order to gain information about the
Japanese that will aid the Americans in their planned efforts to
retake Luzon. The two young pilots not only make contact with

the guerrillas but also rescue their leader, Lieutenant Jackson, from the Japanese and return him to the U.S. fleet. Naturally, they also succeed in releasing all prisoners held by the Japanese garrison.

J172 Emery, Anne [Eleanor McGuigan]. *Tradition*. New York: Vanguard Press, 1946. 250p.

A didactic juvenile story that attempts to promote the acceptance of Japanese-Americans as equal good citizens during the war. The time is 1944 in Northridge, a suburb of Chicago. Two Nisei teenagers, Dorothy and Charlie, move into the community and this is the story of their reception, experiences, and eventual acceptance by most of their peers. A homefront tale that is mainly an account of high school sports, activities, and teenage social life.

J173 Johns, William Earl. *Biggles Delivers the Goods*. London: Hodder and Stoughton, 1946. 182p.

Biggles helps to smuggle strategic rubber out of Japanese-occupied Malaya. Not seen.

J174 Johns, William Earl. *Gimlet Comes Home*. London: University of London Press, 1946. 186p.

This is the last wartime mission of Gimlet. Not seen.

J175 Lansing, Elizabeth Carleton. *Nancy Naylor, Captain of Flight Nurses*. New York: Thomas Y. Crowell, 1946. 241p.

This is one of the titles in a juvenile series of war stories for girls featuring Lt. Nancy Naylor. Nancy is a flight nurse who is now stationed at a bomber base in England. She participates in the D-Day invasion of France, meets up with her fiancé and helps the French resistance in Paris as the Germans retreat. This action is followed by other battlefield and medical flight trips that display Nancy as an eager but somewhat naive creature. At the end she is slightly injured and prepares to return to the States with her fiancé. This is strictly two-dimensional juvenile fare.

J176 Mazet, Horace Sawyer. *Eagles in the Sky*. Philadelphia: Westminster Press, 1946. 189p.

A juvenile story based on the aerial war over the China Sea. The plot covers the harsh conditions and tactical operations of a large night fighter squadron, and the heavy strain on the pilots as a consequence of their combat against the Japanese. Major Shep Graves is the hero of the 78th fighter squadron and narrates this fictional account which concludes when the atomic bomb is dropped on Japan. The text seems a reasonably accurate reflection of the actual conditions.

J177   Montgomery, Rutherford G[eorge]. *Rough Riders Ho!* Philadelphia: David Mckay, 1946. 228p.

The Rough Riders are Sergeant Shorty Teller, Corporal Red Miller, Private Pewee Saunders, Pat O'Rourke, and Private Jerome Gilly. They are part of the U.S. Army's 77th Armored Division and in charge of M-3 and M-6 tanks and half-tracks, about seventy miles from Mainz in Germany. In describing tank combat, the story shows how the Sherman tanks are used for specific jobs against the enemy. The Rough Riders give their tanks unusual names, such as The Little Teddy, Sarah Jane, and Boston Beauty.

J178   Pease, [Clarence] Howard. *Heart of Danger, A Tale of Adventure on Land and Sea with Tod Moran, Third Mate of the Tramp Steamer "Araby."* Garden City, N.Y.: Doubleday, 1946. 336p.

A series juvenile story featuring adventures of Tod Moran. He and Rudy Behrens, a young stoker boy, substitute as secret agents on a confidential mission into German-occupied France. They obtain secret intelligence information from a German officer in Paris who is willing to sell what he can obtain to the Americans. Rudy ends up in Buchenwald for two years before being liberated by the Americans. An action-packed juvenile adventure tale certain to thrill every young reader.

1947

J179   Felsen, Henry Gregor. *Flying Correspondent, A Seth Rantoul Story.* New York: Dutton, 1947. 218p.

A story about the wartime adventures of two young U.S. Marine sergeants in the Pacific theater during the final month of the war. Both men are nineteen. Seth Rantoul works as a reporter and his buddy, Dave Wheaton, is a photographer for the Leatherneck Magazine, the official publication of the Marines. They are traveling by air to the Philippines for a story on dive bombers. The major action of the plot deals with Seth after he is captured and taken by a Japanese boat back to Japan. There he is saved from certain death when the U.S. drops the atom bomb. The story and dialogue are several degrees above the typical boy's war story, especially those about World War I.

J180 Johns, William Earl. *Comrades in Arms*. London: Hodder and Stoughton, 1947. 227p.

Not seen.

J181 McSwigan, Marie. *Juan of Manila*. New York: Dutton, 1947. 152p.

Describes two Filipino boys, Juan and Enrique, who broadcast radio messages of help and resistance to their fellow countrymen during the Japanese occupation. The story relates the patriotic efforts and the persistence of the boys even in the face of enemy searches and the high probability of their capture.

J182 Van der Haas, Henrietta. *Victorious Island*. New York: Harcourt, Brace, 1947. 193p.

A juvenile story about the Dutch inhabitants on the German-occupied island of Walcheren near Antwerp. The time is 1944. The protagonist is Jan de Vries, a fourteen-year-old boy in charge of his family farm. The bombing of the local dikes by the Allies in order to prepare their advance to the mainland, and the impact on Jan and his friends is the major thrust of the novel. The plot places special attention on the courage of the Dutch children who worked with the resistance against the Nazis.

1948

J183 George, Sidney Charles. *Escape From Singapore*. London: Hollis and Carter, 1948. 166p.

An adventure story about David Blake and his parents who are living in Malaya when the Japanese first invade the country in early 1942. David's evil agent is the local Japanese photographer who later appears and reappears as a zealous Japanese Captain after the enemy has occupied all of the surrounding countryside. The plot describes David's adventures and search for his parents, imprisonment by the

Japanese, and repeated rescues. David is sort of a "Jack Armstrong" hero. He and his father are finally reunited before joining his mother in Australia.

J184   Husted, Richard L. *Replacement*. Boston: Meador Publishing Company, 1948. 242p.

This story for older adolescents covers a two-month period in the wartime experiences of an American soldier during the Italian campaign. The novel begins with Bob (whose surname is not given), as troops disembark from a transport ship. In the Naples harbor the infantry replacements are assembled into the Third Infantry Division. In time, the Division is successful in retaking a mountain village from the control of the Germans. Soon Bob becomes more than just the green recruit. He now knows that the men in his "B" Company can always be relied on in combat. Even for a juvenile story the lack of literary style seems all too obvious, e.g., "Bob started moving . . . Bob heard . . . Bob rose . . . Bob hit . . . Bob stopped . . . Bob was . . . Bob had . . . " ad nauseam.

J185   Seredy, Kate. *The Chestry Oak*. New York: Viking Press, 1948. 236p.

The story suggests what the war means to the Hungarian people and to European children in general. The plot traces a young Hungarian prince who escapes from the German occupation and his father's estate of Chestry Valley just before it is destroyed in an air raid in 1944. The narrative shows the effects of the Nazi terror upon the gently-reared, seventeen-year-old Michael, who has lived in a loving and considerate society of caring people. Now, Michael must carry this once-upon-a-time world locked away in his mind. He reaches America and plants an acorn from the Chestry oak of his homeland. An American soldier arranges for the prince to receive his favorite black horse from Hungary. This more than inspires the prince to live up to his past and the traditions of his new country.

J186   Voronkova, Liubov Federovna. *Little Girl From the City*. Translated from the Russian by Josef Berger. Boston: Little, Brown, 1948. 165p. [*Devochka Iz Roroda*. Moscow: 1943. 71p.]

A story about a young Russian refugee girl. When Valya's home in the city is bombed both her mother and baby brother are killed, but she manages to escape to the country where she is adopted by a country family. She quickly learns to adapt to the rougher country ways through her strength of character.

1950

J187   Pashko, Stanley. *Ross Duncan at Bataan*. New York: Messner, 1950. 161p.

This is a short narrative about the Japanese invasion of the Philippines in December of 1941. The American and Filipino resistance and their ultimate defeat at Bataan in April of 1942 is traced through the action of Lt. Ross Duncan and his platoon of Filipino scouts as they fight off Japanese snipers and tanks in miserable jungle conditions. Ross is wounded in the leg and eventually captured and tortured in an enemy prison camp. In spite of his wound, he finally manages to escape into the South China Sea in a small boat where he is rescued by an American sub on its way to Australia. The narrative provides a sketchy idea of what jungle warfare in the Philippines was like when the Japanese swept through the Pacific in the early months of the war.

1952

J188   Bishop, Claire. *Twenty and Ten*. New York: Viking Press, 1952. 76p.

A vivid juvenile tale about twenty French children living in the mountains and cared for by a nun. The time is 1944 in occupied France. One child, Janet, is the narrator. Ten Jewish refugee children turn up and are fed and taken in by the twenty French children and their nun. The story presents with humor and sensitivity the courage of the children under the daily threat of exposure especially when they are visited by German soldiers.

1953

J189   Glemser, Bernard. *Radar Commandos, A Story of World War II*. Philadelphia: Winston, 1953. 180p.

An action juvenile novel about fifteen-year-old Paul Martin, a French boy living in the coastal village of Bruneval. The Germans have built a secret radar installation near the coast in

1941. Paul soon becomes a suspect by the occupying force and joins the local resistance. The narrative tends to alternate between Paul's adventures around Bruneval and British Intelligence activities in England. He helps a British commando team destroy the German radar installation. This is an upbeat inspirational story for young boys.

J190   Lewis, Elizabeth (Foreman). *To Beat a Tiger, One Needs a Brother's Help*. New York: Holt, Rinehart and Winston, 1953. 215p.

Most of the plot takes place in Shanghai during the Japanese occupation. The primary characters are sixteen boys living in a cave-like shack on the outskirts of the International Settlement. The boys from varying backgrounds and social classes are forced to beg and steal in order to survive. They innately sense that only through sharing can they have any hope of survival. The story presents a realistic portrayal of the effect of the war on these young boys as well as the general masses of Chinese. The narrative presents the doctrinal conflict between the Chinese Communists and Nationalists with the sympathy of the author clearly on the side of the Nationalist Chinese. A fast-paced juvenile story that reveals the grim and terrible events that befell the Chinese under the Japanese occupation.

1954

J191   Hunt, Mabel Leigh. *Singing Among Strangers*. Philadelphia and New York: Lippincott, 1954. 213p.

Recounts the experiences of a Latvian family forced to flee both the Russians and the Germans, after losing their elder daughter. The Darzins and their daughters Astra and Dzintra, are transported by the Germans across the Baltic Sea, and then by train and cattle truck to forced labor in Germany. With the coming of the Allies, the family again becomes wanderers. Once again fleeing the Russians, they head for the Western zone under American occupation, where they are housed in Esslingen among their Latvian exiles. By the end of the war, the Darzins happily find a sponsor in the United States.

1955

J192 Bentel, Pearl Bucklen. *I'll Know My Love*. New York: Longmans, Green, 1955. 218p.

A story of twelve-year-old Sirkka Raita and her experiences during the war. With the bombing of her home city of Viipuri by the Russians, Sirkka, her mother and her brother, are ordered to work in an army kitchen. Her father has already been sent to the front. When the battle approaches too close for the family to remain, they are sent as refugees to Lapland. After peace is declared and Finnish land is given to the Russians, the Raitas are re-settled in Helsinki, which is now filled with Nazis. Here Sirkka remains throughout the Nazi occupation of her country.

1956

J193 Bowen, Vernon. *The Emperor's White Horses*. New York: David McKay, 1956. 147p.

Franz Hofer, a young man from the Tyrol, has come into the war-torn city of Vienna in 1945, to search for his parents who were seized by Hitler's secret police. In this almost hopeless search, he finds his cousin Willi, a stableboy in the Spanish Riding School of Lipizzan horses. Franz is also hired at the school, though the school experiences daily bombing. The fate of the horses is pondered daily, but Franz believes that to permit the horses to leave Vienna would be an admission of defeat by the Viennese. The eventual fate of the animals is determined with the help of General George Patton, who gives orders at St. Martin for an American raid through enemy lines to capture the breeding stock of the school. An interesting story for young horse-lovers, by an author whose hobby is writing for young people.

J194 DeJong, Meindert. *The House of Sixty Fathers*. New York: Harper, 1956. 189p.

An account of a Chinese boy, Tien Pao, who lives in Hengyang, but who temporarily loses his father and mother in Japanese-occupied territory. He has been told by his parents to guard the family's sampan while they look for work, but the sampan breaks away from its mooring and flows down with Tien to Japanese-held territory. An American pilot who is shot down by the Japanese is sheltered by Tien. Tien and the pilot manage to walk back at night to the pilot's camp, with the help of Chinese guerrillas. At the camp Tien is well treated by the "sixty fathers" of the Sixteenth Bombardment Squadron, and Tien discovers that his father and mother work in the same camp.

J195   Knight, Clayton. *We Were There at the Normandy Invasion.* New York: Grosset and Dunlap, 1956. 179p.

Another title in this education series on the various war theaters of World War II. The featured character is André, a young French boy who lives with his family on a Normandy farm. André becomes a hero by his fearless help to the Allies when they invade the countryside. The background and facts are authentic which helps create a believable and instructive narrative for juveniles.

J196   Serraillier, Ian Lucien. *The Silver Sword.* London: J. Cape, 1956. 187p. [Also published with the title: *Escape From Warsaw.* New York: Scholastic Book Services, 1963. 218p.]

A juvenile story that traces the impact of the German occupation of Warsaw on the four Balicki children: Ruth, Edek, Bronia, and Jan. The four are treated as representative examples of how the Nazi policies affected children especially when their family home is blown up and their parents taken away to an unknown destination. Ruth, the oldest, is the source of stability and strength as the four are cast adrift in the streets, cellars, fields, and forests as they eventually make their way across war-torn Europe to Switzerland where they hope to locate their parents. The story is apparently based on an actual case very similar to the fictional Balicki family. Well-written, the narrative is filled with suspense and grim realism.

J197   White, Robb. *Up Periscope.* Garden City, N.Y.: Doubleday, 1956. 251p.

This is a better than average naval action story for juveniles. The hero is young Lt. Braden who is given the hazardous mission of being smuggled ashore by a submarine for the purpose of stealing a Japanese code from their shore radio station which is sending top secret data on U.S. military strategy to Japan. The narrative is filled with credible action against a realistic and knowledgeable background of submarine operations.

1957

J198   Appel, Benjamin. *We Were There at the Battle for Bataan.*
New York: Grosset and Dunlap, 1957. 178p.

This is a typical story whose purpose is to inform and
educate young readers about the war in the Philippines. The
time runs from November of 1941 until liberation in July of
1945. The principal characters are Eddie and Diana Beldin
who are fourteen and twelve when the war begins. They live
with their father in Manila and are evacuated to Bataan when
the Japanese invade. The text is the story of their lives as
guerrillas with the Usaffes in the mountains. Diana becomes a
nurse while Eddie is trained to be an active guerrilla soldier.
The text tends to be didactic especially on guerrilla war tactics.
Their father is captured but the two children escape to rejoin
their Usaffe friends. The action covers their daily lives and
experiences during the long war years. Eddie is seriously
wounded and spends months in a hospital. When the islands are
liberated the two children discover happily that their father has
survived as a Japanese POW.

J199   Icenhower, Joseph Bryan. *Submarine Rendezvous: Pacific
Adventure in World War II.* Philadelphia: Winston, 1957.
182p.

A war adventure featuring sixteen-year-old Ben Scott in the
Philippines during early 1942. He is given the special task of
safeguarding the escape from Manila of a scientist whose
information on jungle survival is essential to the Americans in
their war against the Japanese. All of the action is placed in the
Philippines. Unfortunately, the characterization is single-
dimensional with a trite plot permeated with simplistic action
and comic-strip level behavior.

J200   Olsen, Robert I. and David Porter. *Torpedoes Away!* New
York: Dodd, Mead, 1957. 247p.

A story about U.S. submarine warfare ranging from Panama
to Pearl Harbor, and on to the Japanese-controlled waters of
the Philippines and Australia. The authors rely on a formula
approach using a genial but perfectionist captain and an
assortment of crew members. The plot is liberally sprinkled
with comic diversions between naval actions involving depth
charge attacks and the sinking of an enemy oil tanker.

J201   Potter, Jeffrey. *Elephant Bridge*. New York: Viking Press,
       1957. 94p.

       Although the identity of the enemy and the war is not
       specified, it is undoubtedly World War II. The juvenile hero is
       Maung Po from a small Burmese village who wishes he was
       old enough to go to war with his two older brothers even
       though war is evil. He decides to make a trek to the war zone
       and on the way is adopted by a herd of elephants as one of
       their own. This is a rather simple-minded account of his
       adventures with the herd and how he uses these gigantic beasts
       to make a devastating attack on a vital enemy bridge. It is
       difficult to see how this fantasy tale would really benefit any
       child unless a romantic misconception of life in Burma is the
       objective.

J202   Sinclair, Thomas. *We Were There at the Battle of the Atlantic*.
       New York: Grosset and Dunlap, 1957. 139p.

       Not seen.

J203   Sutton, Felix. *We Were There at Pearl Harbor*. New York:
       Grosset and Dunlap, 1957. 177p.

       Tells about the surprise Japanese attack on December 7,
       1941. The scene is described from the point of view of
       fourteen-year-old Mike Morrison whose father, a captain in the
       U.S. Navy, is based at Pearl Harbor. Mike and his Air Force
       pilot brother are sailing in the harbor when the Japanese
       suddenly spring their attack. From that morning until the attack
       ends, Mike helps wherever he can be useful by rescuing men
       from the bay, and saving six sailors who were trapped in their
       sunken ship. He also captures one of the first enemy prisoners
       taken when a badly battered Japanese midget submarine is
       stranded in the bay.

                                1958

J204   Carter, Bruce (pseud.) [Richard Alexander Hough]. *The
       Kidnapping of Kensington: The Children Who Stayed Behind*.
       London: Hamish Hamilton, 1958. 188p. [Republished with
       title: *The Children Who Stayed Behind*. Hamondsworth:
       Penguin, 1964. 154p.]

       A juvenile war fantasy set in Brighton, England in 1940.
       Anticipating invasion at any time the town is evacuated by its

adult inhabitants. The larger war is mirrored in the conflict between three Hartford children and the eight wild Foulsham boys over a small rabbit named Kensington. This leads to various adventures including the encounter of the children with both a German and an English aviator shot down in a dog fight over the town. This is a bizarre combination of real war with juvenile rivalry in a private war among children.

1959

J205   Armstrong, Richard. *The Lame Duck*. London: Dent, 1959. 186p. [Title in U.S.: *Ship Afire! A Story of Adventure at Sea.* New York: John Day, 1960. 188p.]

A juvenile story that tells about an English oil tanker which is torpedoed in the North Atlantic while in a convoy en route to England from Canada. The surviving crew members abandon the ship in a lifeboat. When the captain dies, responsibility for the safety of all the hands falls upon Bull Barlow, a young apprentice seaman who is the hero. Against all odds, he is able to salvage the ship. The narrative is written without any false heroics and with special attention to nautical details.

J206   Forester, Cecil Scott. *The Last Nine Days of the Bismarck*. Boston: Little, Brown, 1959. 138p.

A thinly veiled fictional account of the actual attack, chase, and sinking in 1941 of the powerful German battleship, the *Bismarck*, by British forces. The most charitable reaction would be to characterize the story as a documentary novel. Unfortunately, the dialogue is highly improbable and does not begin to match the description of the sea chase or the facts as employed by the author. The *New Yorker* has provided the best succinct summary and critique: "A short, brisk, Boys' Life account, liberally sprinkled with blood, thunder, and invented conversations."

J207   Knight, Clayton. *We Were There at the Battle of Britain*. New York: Grosset and Dunlap, 1959. 179p.

This is No. 24 in the *"We Were There . . ."* juvenile series of historical novels. This one features fourteen-year-old Alan Lyons and his ten-year-old sister, Cicely and their family friend from America. The story begins with their village war preparations in April of 1940--sandbags, trenches, blackout curtains, etc. Peter, the older brother, joins the RAF. The two children witness and follow the progress of the war into Norway, Luxembourg, France, etc. and participate in the capture of Rudolph Hess when he parachutes into England on his famous peace mission.

1960

J208   Bonham, Frank. *Burma Rifles; A Story of Merrill's Marauders*. New York: Thomas Y. Crowell, 1960. 260p.

This is the story of Jerry Harada, a young California Nisei who is determined to prove himself in combat in Burma. After the placement of his family in a relocation camp, he volunteers for the Army language school and is later sent to India where with thirteen other Nisei volunteers, the group becomes known as Merrill's Marauders. Their mission is to help drive the Japanese troops out of Burma. The story is based on fact and frequently reads almost like a division history of the war. The author also attempts to show the courage and loyalty of Japanese-American citizens in the war. The grimness and misery of jungle warfare are realistically rendered. A sincere albeit didactic juvenile story that stays close to the facts.

J209   Rae, John Malcolm. *The Custard Boys*. London: Rupert Hart-Davis, 1960. 219p.

A novel about a group of thirteen- and fourteen-year-old boys running wild in the Norfolk area of wartime England. It is 1942 and the boys are very much impressed by all the war talk and thus play war games under their own self-devised military code. The narrator is a boy called John who joins a gang led by two rather vicious young toughs. When a new boy called Mark arrives at their school, he is quickly put in the charge of John as a possible recruit for the gang. Since Mark is an Austrian-Jewish refugee from Nazi persecution, he is unable to stay and face the gang's fight challenge to a group of working-class boys. The story attempts to create a parallel between the cruel and aggressive behavior of these young boys and the senseless hate, destruction, and violence of the war.

J210   Strong, Charles Stanley. *The Lost Convoy; Adventure With the Norwegian Underground*. Philadelphia: Chilton, 1960. 194p.

The chief underground leader in Norway, Oskar Carlsen and his fishing boat, are close to being captured by the Germans before Oskar escapes to Lapland with his two sons where they report to commando headquarters for service. Russia needs considerably more supplies since the German bases in Norway have made the Arctic route of the Allies a suicide run. Nevertheless, Carlsen and his crew volunteer to be a part of a supply convoy from Iceland to Murmansk. The narrative captures the flavor of these hazardous journeys through the icy and sub- infested Barents Sea.

1961

J211   Benary, Margot (pseud.) [Margot Benary-Isbert]. *Dangerous Spring*. Translated from the German by James Kirkup. New York: Harcourt, Brace and World, 1961. 252p.; London: Macmillan, 1961. 251p. [*Gefährlicher Frühling*. Hanover: D. Gundert, 1960? 268p.]

An autobiographical novel that describes the experiences of a German doctor's family in eastern Germany during the final days of the war. The heroine is sixteen-year-old Karin Lorenz who has fallen in love with an anti-Nazi pastor twelve years her senior. When the American army occupies the town, Karin serves as a translator and assists in the release of the prisoners in the nearby Buchenwald concentration camp. The plot is well thought out and highly effective in demonstrating that there were conscientious and humane citizens in the Third Reich. This is a superior juvenile story with high quality writing.

J212   Bergamini, David. *The Fleet in the Window, A Novel*. New York: Simon and Schuster, 1961. 378p.; London: Gibbs and Phillips, 1961. 378p.

The major theme of this juvenile story is the Japanese invasion and occupation of the Philippines in 1942. The "Jack Armstrong" hero is Peter Baldwin, the young son of an American missionary doctor stationed there. The Japanese are viewed through Peter's eyes and his experiences which smack too much of the adolescent hero in American juvenile literature. This is also his coming of age emotionally, sexually, and otherwise, just as it is also for his close friends, both male and female. Japanese Colonel Kori is a proper blackguard villain who applies the expected torture, violence, and death by the evil occupying power. Peter ends up fighting for the survival of his own family by joining a group of guerrillas in the hills. He constantly demonstrates bravado and heroism that seems unrealistic, to say the least.

J213   Shepherd, David [Gwynne]. *We Were There at the Battle of the Bulge*. New York: Grosset and Dunlap, 1961. 181p.

Lisa and Adam, two young friends living in the Ardennes Forest, are preparing themselves for the anticipated battle. Lisa has just returned from Bastogne after seeking her father and mother and is now concerned about their conflict of allegiances. Her father is a Belgian doctor who has been helping the Allies while her mother is a German singer who has entertained many soldiers throughout the war. After Adam escapes from Auschwitz he ends up in the German army but has now escaped to join the Americans. Since he is close to the Ardennes Forest, he keeps a division of American troops informed of the plans of the German Army. The use of German paratroopers in American uniforms behind American lines and special techniques such as straw on the roads to muffle the advance of German tanks are all passed on to the Americans by Adam. The narrative provides considerable military detail which may overwhelm many readers.

J214   White, Robb. *Flight Deck*. Garden City, N.Y.: Doubleday, 1961. 215p.

On a small South Pacific island two hundred miles from Guadalcanal, Lt. John Lawrence is grounded by an injury received at Midway. He stations himself alone on the deserted island with a single mission in mind. He will spot Japanese bombers and report their movements with his radio to the Marines on Guadalcanal. The narrative provides ample description of his efforts to reach the island, stay alive, and to accomplish his self-imposed observation and intelligence mission. The story is based on the author's own wartime experiences in the Pacific.

1962

J215   Bonham, Frank. *War Beneath the Sea*. New York: Thomas Y. Crowell, 1962. 263p.

This is a run-of-the-mill story for young adults about submarine warfare. The protagonist is seventeen-year-old Keith Stocker who begins his naval career in Hawaii scarcely two months after the Japanese attack. The action covers 1942 through the end of the war in the Pacific and traces Keith and the other men on the sub as they battle the Japanese underwater throughout the Pacific war zone. The narrative offers a reasonable picture of submarine tactics and life underwater for the younger reader.

J216   Bruckner, Karl. *The Day of the Bomb*. Translated by Frances Lobb. London: Burke Publishing Company, 1962. 189p. [*Sadako will Leben*. Vienna: Verlag fur Jugend und Volk, 1961. 189?p.]

Over one half of this juvenile story describes the circumstances in Hiroshima from July 20, 1945 until the explosion and immediate after effects of the atomic bomb dropped on August 6, 1945. The plot recounts the activities of a number of people including a crippled Japanese boat builder, a young Japanese soldier, the American bomber crew, etc. but especially Shigeo Sasaki and his little sister who are staying in Hiroshima. The last half of the story follows the lives of the two Japanese children over the next ten years when Sadako dies of radiation sickness. The story is most effective in the descriptions covering the effects of the bomb on the people and land of Hiroshima. The character of Sadako Sasaki is regarded in Japan as a veritable Anne Frank figure.

J217   Daniell, David Scott (pseud.) [Alberet Scott Daniell]. *Sandro's Battle*. London: J. Cape, 1962. 158p.; New York: Duell, Sloan and Pearce, 1962. 153p.

A juvenile story placed in Italy and featuring young Allessandro Brozzi called Sandro. He lives with his composer father in an old castle, the Castello della Fontana, which is destined to become a battleground for the opposing British and German forces. Sandro is one who does not take no for an answer especially when protecting his home, his father, or his pet donkey called Anna. When the Germans occupy the castle Sandro slips off to warn the British. This begins his involvement in candlelight signals, partisan activities, sabotage, and various deceptions, even to his father. Naturally, even Anna plays an important role along with Sandro in a final blow to the German army which guarantees victory in Sandro's so-called Battle.

J218   Tunis, John Roberts. *Silence Over Dunkerque*. New York: Morrow, 1962. 215p.

The time is 1940 during the Battle of France when the British forces are pushed into the Channel at Dunkirk. The action is viewed mainly through the eyes of the English Williams family. The father, a sergeant, is with the British

forces on the beach while his family are safe back in England.
When the desperate plight of the men becomes known, the two
twin boys of the sergeant take their small family boat across the
Channel with the rescue flotilla of assorted English boats. The
story describes the difficulties of the small boats as they cross
the rough waters of the Channel. This juvenile story also
describes the fate of a homeless dog adopted by the father and
his men at Dunkirk. This example is symptomatic of what
happens to the dogs of a bombed town during wartime as well
as to children through the person of a young French girl.
Meanwhile the father ends up safe and sound in Calais. This is
a reasonably good description of the Dunkirk evacuation.

J219   Van Stockum, Hilda. *The Winged Watchman*. New York:
       Farrar, Straus and Cudahy, 1962. 204p.

A juvenile story about a Catholic family in Holland during
the German occupation. The year is 1943. The Verhagen
family consists of the parents, two young boys (ten and
fourteen) and their three-year-old sister. Although set during
the occupation with glimpses of persecuted Jews, Resistance
fighters and the hated land-watchers who spied for the Nazis,
the main emphasis is on the devotion and affection of the
Verhagens for one another and their neighbors. There is a
strong implicit point made about their religion being the source
of their strength and love.

J220   White, Robb. *Torpedo Run: Mutiny and Adventure Aboard a
       Navy PT Boat During World War II*. Garden City, N.Y.:
       Doubleday, 1962. 183p.

Another naval story about the war written specifically for
young people and placed in the Far East. This time the plot
covers the mutiny and subsequent action aboard the damaged
and drifting U.S. Navy PT boat, the *Slewfoot*, off the coast of
New Guinea. The story revolves about the consequences of the
new captain who can only operate "by the book." The resultant
deep resentments and mutiny culminates in a test of wills. Of
course, the good guy wins.

                                1963

J221   Armstrong, Richard. *Island Odyssey*. London: Dent, 1963.
       160p. [Title in U.S.: *Fight For Freedom; An Adventure of
       World War II*. New York: McKay, 1966. 150p.]

Here is a realistic juvenile story that is based on a number of
actual incidents in the war. The hero is young seventeen-year-
old Stan, a merchant marine apprentice trapped in Crete when
the Germans cut off the retreat of the British. Stan joins the
trapped British troops in a flight across the island to avoid
capture. He fights with the guerrillas, and finally assumes the
leadership of about 100 men as they take over a dilapidated
landing craft and set sail for North Africa and freedom. There
is a strong anti-war message in this blunt and dramatic fast-
action war tale.

J222   Bateman, Robert. *Race Against the U-boats*. London: J. Cape,
       1963. 111p.

This is an exciting juvenile story that captures some of the
tension and drama caused by the German submarine war
against the shipping between England and Canada. A young
English boy is orphaned early in the war and signs on as a
cabin boy with a tramp steamer in a convoy. This record of his
experiences should hold dramatic interest for most young
readers in search of self-esteem and a wartime adventure to
which they can readily relate.

J223   Forman, James [Douglas]. *The Skies of Crete*. New York:
       Farrar, Straus, 1963. 181p.

This is a vivid, sensitive and reasonably well written juvenile
story about the invasion of Crete by the Germans during the
summer of 1941. The history, people, and patriotic spirit are
represented by the young girl Penny Metaxas, her young
refugee cousin Alexis, and her grandfather Markos as they
react and eventually take a perilous mountain escape trek to the
coast and freedom. The stubborn grandfather at first indulges
in dramatic and misdirected heroics which nearly leads his
family and fellow villagers to destruction. The lesson for
Penny (and presumably the young reader) is that there are no
certainties in war nor are one's loved ones infallible or perfect
under such new and unpredictable circumstances.

J224   Forton, Jean. *The Better Part of Valour*. Translated from the
       French by Alan and Ann-Yvette Stewart. London: J. Cape,
       1963. 290p. [*L'Épingle du Jeu, Roman*. Paris: Librairie
       Gallimard, 1960. 290p.]

The story presents the war in occupied France through the
eyes of a sixteen-year-old French boy, Michel de Pierrefeu,
who is as much concerned with his dislike of the tyranny of his

schoolmaster as he is with the bombing of his town. In the spring of 1944, when the school is closed because of the increased bombing, the schoolmaster persuades Michel and three of his friends to join the resistance group. The four undergo training, rapidly changing from boys to young men. They take part in two successful sabotage raids, and in this they find a worthwhile purpose in their lives, and a friend in the once despised schoolmaster.

J225 Price, Olive M. *The Boy With One Shoe*. New York: Coward-McCann, 1963. 95p.

Mark and Frederick, thirteen-year-old Danish boys, are trained as saboteurs against the German occupation troops in their country. They hate to leave their country when they are to be sent to a British outpost with other Danish children. But instead, they are sent to the Rock of Gibraltar where they discover that their true mission is to contact Sebastian, the king of the smugglers! Naturally, they locate him and then quickly return to Denmark to aid their country in the struggle against the German occupation.

J226 Shemin, Margaretha. *The Little Riders*. New York: Coward-McCann, 1963. 60p.

This is a juvenile tale about a young American girl trapped in Holland at the outbreak of the war. When the German army occupies the country, an enemy officer is quartered in her grandfather's house. The central drama is the effort of Johanna and her grandfather to save the historic lead figures (the little riders) of the town clock tower from being requisitioned for the war effort by the Germans. One of the lessons in this brief story is that the enemy can be viewed as human beings instead of the indiscriminately hated.

J227 Shirreffs, Gordon Donald. *The Cold Seas Beyond*. Philadelphia: Westminster Press, 1963. 192p.

Set in the Aleutian Islands in 1942, this is the juvenile story of Bob Dunbar and his "Irregulars," a ragtag crew of a dependable, but slow diesel ship chartered by the U.S. Government. Their mission is to provide ferry service and supplies to remote military outposts in the Aleutians, as well as engage in salvage operations. Through the long hours aboard ship, the crew becomes a tightly knit group. Their hour of glory finally comes in the cold waters when they meet and defeat a Japanese submarine. A convincing juvenile tale which is the third title in the author's Adventure at Sea series.

J228   Sommerfelt, Aimee. *Miriam.* New York: Criterion Books, 1963. 160p. [*Miriam.* Oslo: Gyldendal, 1960. 135p.]

The setting is Norway in 1941 during the German occupation. The heroine is a young Jewish girl. Her friendship with a Christian girl is the focus of the plot. When Goebbels plans a visit to Oslo the local Germans and their supporters begin a roundup of Jews and other undesirables. The novel explores the treatment of minorities under such circumstances and charts the efforts of the Norwegian underground to help Miriam and some of her family reach the safety of Sweden. This is a fictional treatment that is similar but lacks the impact and power of "The Diary of Anne Frank."

1964

J229   Davis, Franklin M., Jr. *Combat! The Counterattack; A Novel based on the American Broadcasting Co. Television Series.* Racine, WI: Whitman Publishing Company, 1964. 210p.

The time is late 1944 or early 1945. This is a juvenile type story about an American Army squad deep in France and about to enter German territory. The squad encounters a fourteen-year-old war orphan boy called Keeno. Sgt. Saunders suspects him of being a German spy and most of the story revolves about the suspicions and treatment of the boy by the sergeant. When the boy learns the squad will be air dropped by the town where his father is in a prison camp, he stows away aboard one of the gliders and lands with the squad. When the men come under heavy attack by the Germans, the boy saves the day. Saunders apologizes, Keeno finds his father, and there is a happy ending.

J230   Ellis, Leo R. *Nights of Danger.* New York: Funk and Wagnalls, 1964. 123p.

Lee Cole and his widowed mother are living in a small French village during the German occupation. After twelve-year-old Lee decides to translate British news broadcasts for the local one-armed underground leader, he joins a local band of school children who aid the resistance effort by helping with the escape line and supply drops, and trapping a Nazi collaborator. Eventually, the children even blow up a powerful German radio transmitter.

J231   Hale, John. *The Grudge Fight*. London: Collins, 1964. 192p.

The story begins in 1941 and describes a new group of Royal Navy training recruits. It includes two fifteen-year-old boys who become enemies: Brooks from a tough working-class background, and Pike who is secretly atoning for the court martial and suicide of his officer father. The plot is based on the grudge fight tradition of the Royal Navy. These two, however, decide to slug it out at 4:00 a.m. in a deserted room before some of their fellow trainees instead of the supervised three rounds specified in the regulations. The dialogue is typical and coarse British naval lingo that provides, no doubt, an accurate flavor of the early 1940s. This is really a novel about the coming of age of adolescents, and particularly the success of a son where the father has failed.

J232   Harvey, Norman Bruce. *Any Old Dollars, Mister?* Auckland, New Zealand: Paul's Book Arcade, 1964. 155p.; London: Angus and Robertson, 1964. 155p.

A brief story about Reg Jones, an eleven-year-old New Zealand boy, his family, and friends during some of the war years. The time is probably 1942 or 1943. The action occurs in Wellington. This is a homefront story about the social interaction of Reg and a number of Wellington youngsters with the Yanks (mainly Marines and sailors) stationed on the island and preparing for invasion assaults against the Japanese. The point of view is primarily that of the children towards the foreign American military personnel in their midst. The dialogue is in dialect.

J233   Hilton, Irene. *Enemy in the Sky*. Philadelphia: Westminster Press, 1964. 175p.

Bob Foskett, his sister Jane, brother Timmy, and his mother live in London in 1944. His father is in the D-Day invasion. The buzz bombs force the Foskett children to sleep in their cellar. At school, the children must stand in line for their wartime rations. They raise victory gardens while their mother fire-watches at night. One day after school, the children find their home in ruins, with their mother and their brother Timmy killed by a buzz bomb. The children spend that night in a local shelter and are evacuated to the north country for the duration of the war.

J234 McKown, Robin. *Patriot of the Underground*. New York: Putnam, 1964. 192p.

The action takes place in the mining towns of northeastern France during the occupation. When the Germans seize the local men for slave labor elsewhere, many young boys join the underground movement. A group of French boys are called upon by Paul LaCoque to aid their resistance fathers. The fathers of Paul and some of his friends have been seized as hostages following the sabotage of a coal train. Since the boys know their elders are resistance members, they contact the leaders of the local resistance and volunteer to help. The story demonstrates that even young boys in desperate times can carry the responsibilities of adults.

J235 Mcleod, Grover Stephen. *Sub Sailor*. Birmingham, AL: Manchester Press, 1964. 315p.

Describes life aboard an American submarine while the crew patrol the seas from northern Japan to Australia. The story features a young sailor called Robert Ham from Alabama, who is on his first sea duty. After testing torpedoes, the submarine enters enemy waters in the Sea of Japan and travels to the China Sea, Australia, and then back to the Philippines attacking enemy shipping.

J236 Meynier, Yvonne. *The School with a Difference*. Translated from the French by Patricia Crampton. London: Abelard-Schuman, 1964. 159p. [*Un Lycée Pas Comme les Autres*. Paris: Société Nouvelles des Éditions G.P., 1962. 186p.]

A juvenile story cast in the form of a series of letters to and from a mother and her two daughters and covering the period from September 1943 through July of 1944. The place is occupied France. The country is divided into two sections: one occupied by the Germans and the other by the Vichy regime. The two girls are at an evacuated school in the country while the mother and her youngest daughter are in the town of Rennes. The author has based the story on her own experiences during the war. The plot presents the tension and fears of daily life in an enemy-occupied country. This story received the Grand Prix de la Literature pour les Jeunes in France. The work is now considered a piece of documentary fiction.

J237 Senje, Sigurd (pseud.) [Sigurd Rasmussen]. *Escape!*. Translated from the Norwegian by Evelyn Ramsden. New

York: Harcourt, Brace and World, 1964. 156p. [*Stepans Skrin.*]

After the German invasion and occupation of Norway, two fourteen-year-old classmates, Ingred and Elling, are forced to move with their families from the coast to an inland valley. They join an underground group which assists a young Russian prisoner to escape from the Nazis and reach safety in neutral Sweden. This is a juvenile story that begins at a plodding pace but later develops some fast action and suspense.

J238   Shirreffs, Gordon Donald. *The Hostile Beaches*. Philadelphia: Westminster Press, 1964. 192p.

This is a typical juvenile war story placed in the South Pacific. Bob Dunbar and Gary Lunt are buddies on a U.S. destroyer. There is plenty of fast action about naval battles at sea, mines, and PT boat attacks on enemy supply barges. This is adventure reading for boys which provides a fairly realistic sense of the actual war at sea and on land in the Solomon Islands behind Japanese lines with the two heroes. It is the second title of the Adventure at Sea series of the author.

J239   Werstein, Irving. *The Long Escape*. New York: Scribner, 1964. 189p.

A story based on a real life incident that occurred in Belgium. The events take place primarily during May 10 to June 2, 1940, the period covering the successful Dunkirk evacuations by the British. The focus of the story is on fifty rest-home children and Justine, their director, all of whom become refugees when the Germans invade Belgium on May 10. They are traced as they eventually escape to Dunkirk where they are taken to England. The story is especially notable for capturing the helplessness and panic of the refugees. The descriptions of the blazing and exploding French port is much like a scene from Dante's *Inferno*. The emphasis of this story is on the plight of children as refugees in time of war.

J240   White, Robb. *The Survivor*. Garden City, N.Y.: Doubleday, 1964. 204p.

A melodramatic juvenile story about a secret mission for which the hero, a young Navy pilot, is literally conscripted against his wishes. He is ordered to a submarine and joins a crack platoon of marines in order to scout a Japanese-held atoll. The reader gets a reasonably good impression of the humid, cramped life aboard an underwater vessel. Adam, the pilot, is described as he overcomes his resentment and finally performs an act of heroism after the sub is disabled. The story concludes with a flurry of military action with the Japanese, all calculated to instill patriotic fervor and pride.

1965

J241 Chamberlain, William. *Matt Quarterhill, Rifleman*. New York: John Day, 1965. 187p.

Describes the experiences of Private Quarterhill and the men of his squad during the assault of their forces on the Japanese mountain strongholds in Leyte. This is the story of a closely knit group of men and their reactions to each other in combat as they attempt to rout the enemy entrenched in their concealed caves and bunkers. Although a juvenile account of the war in the Philippines, its depiction of the devastating island warfare might well interest adult readers.

J242 Holm, Anne S. *North to Freedom*. Translated from the Danish by L.W. Kingsland. New York: Harcourt, Brace and World, 1965. 190p. [*David*. Kφbenhavn: Gyldendal, 1963. 155p.]

A twelve-year-old Danish boy by the name of David has lived most of his short life in a prison camp in eastern Europe. He escapes with only the instruction that he must find his way to Denmark. From a repressive environment of suspicion and distrust of all others, he is suddenly forced out into a world where he must relearn all of the normal human feelings and reactions. From an Italian port in the south of Italy he sets out on foot across Europe. This journey also constitutes a trip of discovery or rediscovery of his own identity which has been repressed during all the years of prison camp life. The author stretches the historical facts when she creates the impression of an almost carefree and peaceful European countryside as a contrast to the suspicions and restrictions of prison camp existence. This juvenile novel was the winner of the 1963 Gyldendal Prize for the best Scandinavian children's book.

J243 Middleton, Jan. *Learn to Say Goodbye*. New York: Dodd, Mead, 1965. 184p.

This juvenile story focuses on an army nurse. Judith Morgan has volunteered for duty at an evacuation hospital in the

Algerian desert. The narrative provides vivid descriptions of the long, desperate days of the North African campaign and its interminable stream of casualties. Judith volunteers to serve in a combat zone, hoping to forget a double tragedy, the death of her pilot fiancé and of her brother. Eventually Judith's superior, Captain Christie, becomes her new love interest.

J244   Sentman, George Armor. *Russky*. Garden City, N.Y.: Doubleday, 1965. 176p.

Traces the adventures of a fifteen-year-old Russian boy, Pyotr Dmitrievich Pribylov, who has escaped from a German labor camp east of the Rhine and hides in a deserted French barn. When he is discovered by American soldiers, Pyotr is nicknamed "Russky" and becomes the mascot of OBIE Company. Though he is given KP duty behind the lines, he witnesses plenty of action. The time is 1945, and it is bitter cold in January as the American infantry tries desperately to wipe out the German resistance in Alsace. The battle scenes are realistic and fast-paced. Much of this narrative is based on the personal experiences of the author.

J245   Shirreffs, Gordon Donald. *The Enemy Seas*. Philadelphia: Westminster Press, 1965. 190p.

Early in the war Bob Dunbar and Gary Lunt, two young American sailors, are swept overboard from their destroyer during a storm. Rescued by a sub near Brisbane, they are now involved in the secret missions of the submarine as it penetrates deep into Japanese- controlled waters. The plot covers nearly every aspect of life on a sub--from placing depth charges and attacks on the Japanese fleet to commando raids on an enemy-held island. The story has the usual narrow escapes and acts of heroism. This is a somewhat didactic adventure tale for juveniles and the first title in the author's Adventure at Sea series for juveniles.

J246   Stow, Randolph. *The Merry-go-round in the Sea*. London: Macdonald, 1965. 283p.

A leisurely paced homefront novel placed in Australia during and after the war. About half of the story occurs during the war years. Six-year-old Rob is evacuated from his seacoast home to a sheep farming station towards the interior of the continent. Rob has a deep affection and case of hero worship for his cousin Rick who goes off to fight the Japanese. The narrative is from the point of view of Rob, his childish perceptions, problems, activities, and fears for the safety of his cousin in the war. Rob is surrounded by his extended family of aunts, cousins, and grandparents as the war years pass and Rick is taken prisoner by the Japanese in Malaya. Mainly, the story is the account of Rob's coming of age which happens to take place during the war.

1966

J247   Chamberlain, William. *Murphy Higheagle, Paratrooper*. New York: John Day, 1966. 192p.

It is the eve of the Allied invasion at Normandy. Murphy Higheagle, the grandson of a Cherokee chief, is ordered to be rotated home due to his many bombing missions over Europe and his war wounds. He refuses and manages to arrange a transfer from the Air Force to an airborne infantry unit in England where he is to take over as a platoon leader. The narrative describes his eventual acceptance into the airborne and his adventures in the French hedgerow country inland from the invasion beaches. He and his men take over a German-held town by capturing enemy tanks and rescuing a French woman and her grandfather. Under the leadership of Murphy, the unit sets out to harass the superior enemy forces. This is standard juvenile war story material emphasizing the effectiveness of American Indians in combat and leadership.

J248   Daly, Maureen [Mrs. William Peter McGivern]. *The Small War of Sergeant Donkey*. New York: Dodd, Mead, 1966. 85p.

Tells the story of the relationship between Chico, a young Italian boy, and Sergeant John Price from Missouri who is known as Sergeant Missouri. At the time the story begins, the war has moved northward, leaving southern Italy even more impoverished than before the war. Farms have been plundered, farm animals killed, and the people's beast of burden, the burros, have been taken away by the Germans. Sergeant Missouri is in charge of collecting and herding the donkeys captured from the retreating Germans as well as those imported from the U.S. and Africa. Chico falls in love with one small North African donkey with a broken leg and often goes to the American encampment to visit the donkey and Sergeant Missouri. Chico is instrumental in saving Sergeant Missouri when he is pinned down by German fire and is given the donkey as a reward.

J249   Levin, Jane Whitbread. *Star of Danger*. New York: Harcourt, Brace and World, 1966. 160p.

A juvenile story about two Jewish boys who are successfully smuggled to neutral Sweden. Eighteen-year-old Karl and his close friend, Peter, previously had to flee Germany in 1939. This time they are living in Denmark in 1943 when the Nazis begin to arrest all the Jews. This is the story of their escape through the efforts of the resistance. The novel seems a good account of how the Danish underground works, its complexity, and the intricacy of the planning at all levels. It also shows the concern of the ordinary Danes and Swedes who also risked their lives to save the Jews.

J250   Shirreffs, Gordon Donald. *The Bolo Battalion*. Philadelphia: Westminster Press, 1966. 218p.

This title continues the wartime adventures of Bob Dunbar and Gary Lunt. This time they are back in the Philippines on their second patrol with the guerrilla forces under orders from General MacArthur to support covertly the future Allied invasions by harassing the Japanese in every way possible. This is a fairly realistic jungle combat description with plenty of excitement for the juvenile reader. It is the fourth title in the Adventure at Sea series featuring these two boy heroes.

J251   Stiles, Martha Bennett. *Darkness over the Land*. New York: Dial Press, 1966. 269p.

A juvenile story about a German family in Munich during the war. The young protagonist is only nine when the war begins in 1939. All of his teachers and the times praise Hitler, of course, and denounce the enemies of the Reich: Jews, Slavs, Catholics, etc. This is essentially a tale of his confusion between the official line of the state and the private opinion of his parents. Pushed to join the Nazi *Jungvolk* he later sees his uncle arrested and his brother forced into military service. His gradual awakening results in his help to the "White Rose" student resistance group in Munich. The narrative straightforwardly describes the grisly effects of the Allied bombings and the brutality not only of the Nazis but also by the Allied occupying forces when they find the concentration camp of Dachau. This is a frank picture of the misery and chaos brought about by the war on the Germans as well as a revealing account of how it was to grow up in Nazi Germany, an interesting theme for a juvenile novel.

J252 Visser, William Frederick Hendrik. *Gypsy Courier*. Edinburgh: Oliver & Boyd, 1966. 187p.;Chicago: Follett, 1966. 187p. [*Niku de Koerier*. The Hague: Van Goor Zonen, 1964. 190p.]

This is an intriguing and thoughtful narrative about the activities of the underground Polish Army in the Warsaw area from about May to November of 1944. The action focus is presented through the character of Niku Kropan, a fifteen-year-old gypsy boy from Warsaw. He becomes a courier for the Polish underground army but soon also becomes a capable saboteur of German controlled records which list the Polish farms crop production and the names of hundreds of Polish men and boys from the surrounding areas. Niku soon meets up with another gypsy boy, Victor, and they quickly find themselves back in Warsaw in the midst of the uprising. Niku is wounded in the arm but both boys join up with Captain Sikorski and his army in fighting the Germans and defending the ghetto Jews, particularly a brother and sister, David and Ruth. When Sikorski and his men decide to surrender to the Germans, Niku, Victor and David are encourage to escape into the countryside to safe houses and individuals. This they decide to do as the story ends. The narrative is a well written testament to the resistance of the Poles and the bravery and character of the gypsies and Jews.

J253 White, Robb. *Surrender*. Garden City, N.Y.: Doubleday, 1966. 240p.

A juvenile adventure tale covering the days immediately after Pearl Harbor and the surrender of the Philippines. The plot describes the five-month escape trek of a homeless Filipino-American boy and girl, an American civilian, and a U.S. Navy officer in their resourceful efforts to avoid capture by the Japanese. They undergo starvation, strafing, and all of the nightmare effects of disease and the constant fear of capture, torture and death. This is a fairly realistic exposure to the horrors of war for young people.

J254 Wingate, John [Allan]. *Never So Proud: Crete, May 1941: The Battle and Evacuation*. London: Heinemann, 1966. 212p.

A fictionalized account of the battle and evacuation of Crete during ten days in May 1941. Three of the major characters are clearly fictional while the rest are based on actual British participants in the conflict. The narrative traces the fate of the British Mediterranean fleet and the disastrous Crete campaign moment by moment throughout the crisis. In spite of the mass of characters and action the story effectively connects one incident to another with suspense. Most of the story is related through the eyes of two naval airmen who become separated when their aircraft is shot down but are later reunited at the retreat. This is an obvious historical narrative intended for juveniles but since it constantly fluctuates between fact and fiction it has been classified by some libraries as nonfiction.

1967

J255   Bonnell, Dorothy. *Passport to Freedom*. New York: Julian Messner, 1967. 191p.

This is an inept and heavy-handed juvenile adventure story about the various efforts of an American girl to escape from occupied France after her passport is stolen. It is the summer of 1940. Sally Schmidt is a student at the Sorbonne in Paris when the Nazis take over the city. She joins the stream of refugees flowing into unoccupied Marseilles in her attempts to go back to the States. She is trapped in incredible red tape and bureaucratic obstacles. Even when she manages to leave by boat the craft capsizes and she ends up again in German-occupied French territory. At the end, however, she successfully escapes with the promise of a future romantic involvement.

J256   Forman, James. *Horses of Anger*. New York: Farrar, Straus and Giroux, 1967. 249p.

In the last weeks of the war, Hans Amann, the fifteen-year-old protagonist, has been ordered along with about fifty other boys in a German anti-aircraft battery to defend a jet factory. The boys recognize that their guns cannot hit any of the British and American bombers. Through flashbacks, Hans is followed from his days of dedication to the Nazi cause, to his present disgust for Hitler and all he stands for, which causes him to welcome the defeat of Germany. His friend Siegfried still holds to Hitler's promises while his uncle, a professional soldier, is as horrified as Hans, and attacks SS troops in Munich. The narrative is a good impression of how it was like in Germany through the war years for boys like Hans. The story seems uncompromising in its integrity especially in regard to historical details. The last five pages present a glossary of individuals' names, slogans, and organizations connected with the Third Reich.

J257   Hardy, William Marion. *U.S.S. Mudskipper, The Submarine That Wrecked a Train*. New York: Dodd, Mead, 1967. 216p.

The protagonist is U.S. Navy Commander Tolliver who has been plying the Hokkaido coast of Japan. Even though he has not seen any enemy shipping for weeks, he is starting to fall apart from the strain of war duty. He decides to destroy a freight train he has seen along the shore, running daily between Nemuro and Kushiro. When he and some of the crew turn themselves into a landing force, Tolliver is killed minutes before the train is bombed. Unfortunately, the characters are stereotypes and artificial in construction.

J258   Haugaard, Erik Christian. *The Little Fishes*. Boston: Houghton Mifflin, 1967. 214p.

This is the story of a twelve-year-old boy called Guido who lives as a beggar in the streets of Naples. He is representative of all those abandoned Italian children of the war years who were caught between the Axis and Allied armies in Italy. His spirit and resourcefulness enable him to survive along with two other street children: Mario who eventually dies from illness, and Anna who becomes a sister in spirit as they decide to stay together and continue their hapless journey, ever hopeful of finding a real home. The title *Little Fishes* refers to these lost and wandering children. This is a touching and memorable human interest story that is written in a poetic and sensitive manner.

J259   Shirreffs, Gordon Donald. *Torpedoes Away*. Philadelphia: Westminster Press, 1967. 206p.

This is a continuation of the adventures of Bob Dunbar and Gary Lunt aboard the *Grayfin*, a U.S. submarine operating in the Japanese-controlled waters of the South Pacific during the last year of the war. Their chief mission is to seek out and sink a mysterious enemy Q-ship and its accompanying German submarine. The *Grayfin* sinks the Q-ship in the Java Sea while a U.S. destroyer in the same area attacks what appears to be an old freighter, but which turns out to be a cleverly disguised Q-ship. This is the fifth and last title in the author's Adventure at Sea series for boys.

J260   Tunis, John R[oberts]. *His Enemy, His Friend*. New York: William Morrow, 1967. 196p.

Slightly more than half of this juvenile story takes place during the occupation of France. The main character is Hans von Kleinschrodt, a young German soldier (and later a champion soccer player) who is ordered to kill six hostages in the village where he is stationed. He refuses to kill the local people who have become his friends. All the same, after the war at a war crimes trial he is accused of being the killer. He is sentenced to prison for ten years as a result of his inability to prove he had refused the order. The rest of the story takes place twenty-five years later. Hans again meets the French, but in a soccer game. This time in an ironic twist, the citizens of Nogent-Plage take six German players as hostages. The basic theme is the futility of hatred and revenge. An unusually effective anti-war story.

J261   Walsh, Jill Paton. *The Dolphin Crossing*. London: Macmillan, 1967. 134p.; New York: St. Martin's Press, 1967. 134p.

The plot traces two boys in Kent, England in 1940. John Astor comes from an upper-class family; Pat is an evacuee from a London slum. In spite of the class differences, the two boys grow together as a strong working team by helping in the war effort. Their most important service in the war is to help in the evacuation of British soldiers at Dunkirk, using John's small boat. This juvenile story also touches on rationing and the black market in England during the war.

J262   White, Robb. *Silent Ship, Silent Sea*. Garden City, N.Y.: Doubleday, 1967. 231p.

Straight out of boot camp and bound for officer candidate school in Rhode Island, Kelsey Devereux is inadvertently assigned to sea duty aboard an ill-fated destroyer. The ship soon has an encounter with a submarine, is damaged by a typhoon, and is severely crippled during an invasion in the Solomon Islands when a Japanese plane crashes into its deck. The vessel is salvaged by the Japanese who are unaware that Kelsey and the captain are still aboard and alive. The narrative seems to be filled with plenty of realistic sea action.

1968

J263   Balderson, Margaret. *When Jays Fly to Barbmo*. London: Oxford University Press, 1968. 202p.

Ingeborg Nygaard, a girl in her teens who is half Norwegian and half Lapp, lives with her father and her aunt in a small Norwegian seashore village. One morning she spots a German ship off the coast, and shortly the country is under the German occupation. Her father has been transporting Norwegian soldiers on his fishing boat, and when he refuses to stop, his boat is sunk with no survivors. Soon a swastika is hoisted above the community hall, farmers are forced to give up large portions of their stored food, local people are imprisoned, school is closed, and any uncooperative students are sent to labor camps. Eventually when the Germans prepare to retreat due to the Russian advance, the Nazis decide to burn the village to keep it from the Russians. Ingeborg leaves her family home and skis north to be with her Lapp friends. This is a well written story about how a young Norwegian girl recognizes what war really means, how she learns to react to adversity, and how to deal with the presence of the enemy.

J264 Bernhardsen, Christian [Einar Christian Rosenvinge Bernhardsen]. *The Fight in the Mountains*. Translated from the Danish by Franey Sinding. New York: Harcourt, Brace and World, 1968. 128p. [*Kampen pa Fjeldet*. Gyldendal, 1966.]

Here is a forthright and deadly serious juvenile story placed in the closing days of the war. A young Norwegian and two friends flee into the mountains to join up with the Free Norwegian Forces. They help in blowing up oil tankers and trains and eventually become involved in a furious fight to defend their mountain stronghold from a determined German attack. There is a grim realism here that captures the impersonality of death, Nazi terrorism, resistance retaliation, the tense and suspenseful nature of sabotage efforts, and the self-destructiveness of hatred. This is a serious attempt to acquaint young readers with the real nature of war.

J265 Bonham, Frank. *The Ghost Front*. New York: Dutton, 1968. 223p.

This juvenile story traces the experiences of two American soldiers, one who is in the "Golden Lions" unit of the 106th Infantry Division and the other in the Second Infantry Division. The soldiers are eighteen-year-old twins, Tom and Andy Croft. The twins become separated, contrary to the Army's promises, when Andy is shipped out while Tom is recovering from a wounded foot. The twins try to find each other, but meanwhile the German Army, presumed to be in retreat after the

Normandy invasion, launches a counter-offensive which breaks through the thin American defense. Moving from one twin to the other, the author shows how each boy learns to function on his own. This is a realistic picture of the Battle of the Bulge for young readers.

J266   Burland, Brian. *A Fall from Aloft*. London: Barrie and Rockcliff, 1968. 195p.

This is a psychological study of early adolescence with particular emphasis on the sexual coming of age of a thirteen-year-old boy called James Berkeley. He is a young English boy who is sent to England by his parents on a midwinter voyage in 1942. He is a passenger on a freighter which is part of a convoy taken across the Atlantic at the height of the German U-boat attacks. The story of the sea journey and the ever present day-by-day fear and terror of the crew over an attack are the background tensions of James' rite of passage into adolescence. There is a considerable amount of British slang and obscenities in the dialogue. Interspersed with the descriptions of the rigors and the problems of James are intermittent flashbacks into his family life and previous personal activities. The flavor of a wartime convoy sea journey is undoubtedly captured with considerable realism. The author has no hesitation in calling a spade a spade, whether human excrement or vomit, in this traumatic journey into early adulthood.

J267   Burton, Hester. *In Spite of All Terror*. London: Oxford University Press, 1968. 183p.

Presents in documentary fashion the events in England during the first year of the war through the experiences of a fifteen-year-old orphan girl, Elizabeth Hawtin. Along with her classmates she is evacuated in September of 1939 from the London slums to Oxfordshire in the country where she is introduced to a very different life from the one she had previously known. She learns to love her new temporary family, the aristocratic Breretons, and becomes a part of their life. With one of the sons and his grandfather, she helps in the evacuation of soldiers from Dunkirk when the Brereton's yacht is commandeered. She rejoices with the family when they receive word that their older son, formerly listed as missing, is instead a prisoner of war. The story is basically autobiographical and features an engaging contrast of Cockney and Oxonian speech as the two different cultures and vocabularies interact.

J268 Clarke, John (pseud.) [Càrli Laklan]. *Black Soldier*. Garden City, N.Y.: Doubleday, 1968. 144p.

Here is an honest and forthright juvenile story about the wartime circumstances of black soldiers in the U.S. Army. George Bunty, the hero, is eager to fight for his country but quickly discovers, along with others of his race, that he is also a second-class citizen as a soldier no matter his ability or intelligence. George is followed through basic training, special desert training, and finally when he is sent overseas to England and combat in Europe. All of these experiences are filled with instances and examples of discrimination, usually by white officers and troopers. Blacks are segregated in their own companies and units much to their disappointment and dismay. This is a simple narrative about the place, behavior and treatment of blacks in the European war covering such battles as the D-Day invasion and the Battle of the Bulge.

J269 Forman, James Douglas. *The Traitors*. New York: Farrar, Straus and Giroux, 1968. 238p.

The story deals with the fortunes of the Eichhorn family in Nazi Germany from about 1938 to 1945. The father, Gottfried, is an Evangelical pastor who is still in mourning for his dead wife. His chief comfort is a foundling son called Paul who becomes dearer to him than his real son, Kurt, who is a Nazi. The major theme is about growing up in Germany but growing up as an individual who must take a stand against the practices of a corrupt state. As the Nazi power grows and leads to a prolonged war, not only is the pastor father led to speak out but also young Paul who attempts to hide a Jewish friend from the Germans. Ultimately, they both make a desperate effort to aid the advancing American army as it approaches Ravenskirch. This is one of a number of unusual juvenile stories that realistically explore how life really was in Nazi Germany during the war.

J270 Styles, [Frank] Showell. *Indestructible Jones*. New York: Ives Washburn, 1968. 148p.

David Jones, the protagonist, enlists in the Royal Navy but with misgivings because he believes that no one has the right to kill another. Assignment to a minesweeper seems to satisfy his scruples, since such a craft does not make murderous attacks. On board the ship his understanding friend, Petty Officer Bott, uses a rule of thumb to cover the situation of David: "Us pacifists won't do no good till it's over. We got to fight, son, an' fight with all we got." Confirmation of this homely dictum comes with the sinking of the ship. Thus begins the military career of David. When Jones and Bott go to Dunkirk and to Tobruk to pick up captured guns for unarmed British merchant vessels and return unharmed, Jones earns the title of "Indestructible Jones." This is a pedestrian story with many of David's experiences improbable and hard to believe.

1969

J271   Clagett, John. *Torpedo Run on Iron Bottomed Bay*. New York: Cowles Book Company, 1969. 168p.

Here is an antiseptic and bowdlerized juvenile story about the Battle of Guadalcanal from the perspective of a young PT boat sailor who demonstrates considerable patriotism and Naval esprit de corps. The main theme is duty above all else. There are the usual battle scenes with death and injury, but the honest reality of wartime experience seems to escape the narrative and the characterization.

J272   Haar, Jaap Ter. *Boris*. Translated from the Dutch by Martha Mearns. London: Blackie, 1969. 152p. [*Boris*. Bussum: Van Holkema and Warendorf, 1966. 158p.]

A short juvenile novel about a young boy of twelve who experiences the German siege of Leningrad in 1942. Nearly starving, Boris goes with a friend to forage for potatoes in a forbidden zone. They run into several German soldiers who feel sorry for their plight and feed them. Afterwards the soldiers use a white flag to guide them back to the Russian lines. Boris and his friend who had always been taught to hate the Germans now realize that the real victims of war are the ordinary citizens. Obviously, this is a juvenile story with the message of forgiveness. The writing is extremely well done and sensitive without being sentimental.

J273   Olson, Gene. *Drop Into Hell*. Philadelphia: Westminster Press, 1969. 156p.

Here is a somewhat unusual teenager novel. It clearly reveals the dissatisfaction of the soldiers with the war. There is no glamour or romance. What comes across is the futility, frustration, and hopelessness of war. The plot describes the advance preparation for the pre-invasion of Utah beach on the nights of June 5 and 6, 1944. It turns out to be a disaster of mismanagement and faulty military intelligence. The protagonist is Private Carlson but the characters are mainly known only by name, rank and serial number. Nonetheless, Carlson and his buddy do their part in spite of their doubts and deep misgivings.

J274   Prince, Alison. *The House on the Common*. London: Methuen, 1969. 142p.

The time is 1942 in England. Two children, Jane and Derek, think the older Liepmann couple who speak German are really spies. After a series of ridiculous if not absurd events at night during the blitz, they discover that the old couple are really Jewish refugees. The sketches by the wife are illustrations for children's books; not for the enemy. The theme is how easily uninformed minds can be subject to prejudice and jingoism in wartime.

J275   Taylor, Theodore. *The Cay*. Garden City, N.Y.: Doubleday, 1969. 137p.

A relatively short juvenile story placed in the middle years of the war. Philip, an eleven-year-old boy, is being taken back to the United States by his mother on a freighter when the ship is torpedoed by a German sub. Philip finds himself blinded by a blow to his head and very much alone on a raft with a huge, ugly old Negro. The two are cast up on a small barren Caribbean island where Philip has all the racial prejudices of his childhood dispelled under the considerate and wise care of the old West Indian black. The racial theme is the major purpose of this book but it is presented in such an unobtrusive way that there is no sense of sermonizing or didacticism.

J276   Vivier, Colette. *The House of the Four Winds*. Translated . . . by Miriam Morton. Garden City, N.Y.: Doubleday, 1969. 190p. [*La Maison des Quatre-vents*. Paris: Société Nouvelles des Éditions, 1965. 187p.]

A juvenile story set in German-occupied Paris during 1943. The plot reveals what it was like to live then by using a potpourri of French individuals living in an apartment house. The main focus is on twelve-year-old Michel who dreams of joining the French underground. The rest of the residents consist of two timid spinsters, a Jewish family in hiding, relatives of resistance workers, etc. and a family of collaborators, hated by all the others. The story relates how all of the residents become involved in the struggle before the Allied liberation. The writing is competent and often vivid.

J277   Walsh, Jill Paton. *Fireweed*. London: Macmillan, 1969. 140p.

Two youngsters meet in London. Bill is with a group of young people being evacuated to Wales, and Julie's parents are putting her on a ship going to Canada. These two insist on staying together, and together they explore London with streets torn up by large holes, burning buildings, and bombings every night. As the days go by, they maintain a regular program, working in the market stalls in the daytime, and sleeping in underground stations at night. Ultimately, with money that Julie has, the two make a clandestine home of sorts in torn-up London, ill prepared as they are for communal life. Though this is a story of and for juveniles, it is a well plotted novel, especially about London during the blitz.

1970

J278   Cooper, Susan. *Dawn of Fear*. New York: Harcourt, Brace, Jovanovich, 1970. 157p.

A juvenile story placed in London during the blitz. Derek, only eleven years old, and his friends Geoff and Peter seem more preoccupied with their special secret camp site than the daily German air raids or the RAF efforts to intercept them. War for the children is mainly conflict with a neighboring gang when they attempt to defend their secret camp. It is obvious that the author wishes to connect the cruelty and hate of the White Road boys' gang with the larger issue of the hate and cruelty that result from war. The lesson becomes especially obvious when Peter's home is destroyed by a German bomb-- along with all the family. This is a subtle story that confronts the issue of death and loss.

J279   Grund, Josef Carl. *Never to be Free: A Novel*. Translated by Lucile Harrington. Boston: Little, Brown, 1970. 202p. [*Flakhelfer Briel*. Nüremburg: Sebaldus, 1965. 172p.]

The desperate German need for manpower near the end of the war causes Germany to enlist sixteen-year-old boys into the army. Twelve such boys are described through the narrative of one of the group, Gustav Briel. At first Briel is a believing Hitler Youth in charge of an anti-aircraft gun-emplacement. But later when the bombings are daily, with close friends dead and wounded, many of the older gunners and their superiors develop serious reservations about the Nazi Party, and Gustav becomes completely disillusioned with the country. This theme is handled convincingly by the author.

J280 Kumin, Maxine [Winokur]. *When Mother was Young.* New York: Putnam, 1970. 64p.

When Maggie Corcoran grew up in Brooklyn, she bought defense stamps at school, stood in line for ration stamps, picked up rubber, cardboard, scrap metal, tin cans, pots and pans for the war effort, and took care of the family's victory garden. When she married, her husband went in the Navy and she worked in the Brooklyn Naval Yard in the shipbuilding section. The narrative is a catalog of wartime activities in the city for both children and adults.

J281 Neshamit, Sarah. *The Children of Mapu Street, A Novel.* Translated from the Hebrew by David S. Segal. Philadelphia: Jewish Publication Society of America, 1970. 324p. [*Ha-Yeladim Me-Rehov Mapu.* 1968. 73p.]

It is the eve of the German invasion of Russia in 1941. The story begins in the capital of Lithuania where the residents undergo one brutal incident after another: children shot, anti-Semitic looting, forced separation of families, etc. as viewed through the eyes of a group of uncomprehending children. Gradually the story focuses on two of the children: Shula, the teen-aged daughter of a doctor, and Shmulik, the twelve-year-old son of a tailor. Originally neighbors, they soon are separated in the fighting and only are reunited at the end of the novel. Shula's mother is killed and she finds sanctuary in a convent where the anti-Semitic abbess offers her conversion to Catholicism. In contrast, Shmulik escapes from a death camp train and joins the partisans. After plenty of heroics, the girl and boy again meet and set off for a new life in Israel. The narrative is uncomplicated and simple with an upbeat but rather contrived ending.

J282 Wayne, Kyra Petrovskaya. *Shurik. A Story of the Siege of Leningrad.* New York: Grosset and Dunlap, 1970. 209p.

This is the story of a Russian nurse and an orphan boy, both trapped in Leningrad by the German Army during the three-year siege. Kyra, serving as a military nurse, finds Shurik in the ruins of his family's bombed building. The story describes the efforts of these two to survive during the siege. Shurik becomes a hero at a Leningrad military hospital, leading forty-one wounded soldiers to safety when the hospital is bombed by German planes. The major theme is the suffering and heroism of the Leningrad people.

1971

J283   Kerr, Judith. *When Hitler Stole Pink Rabbit*. London: Collins, 1971. 191p.

In 1933 nine-year-old Anna discovers that her father is missing and that her mother and her brother Max must quickly leave Berlin for Switzerland. The change has something to do with an election the Nazis have won. Just choosing a stuffed dog or a pink rabbit to take with her is difficult for Anna. When all of the family is reunited in Switzerland they soon learn to adjust to new languages and new homes; how to be poor; and how to develop the special skills of a refugee. As the family moves from Switzerland to France and then to England, Anna realizes that she will never again see Germany and the stuffed rabbit she left behind. This is a perceptive picture of a child's world, especially how small matters frequently overshadow large issues.

J284   Oneal, Zibby. *War Work*. New York: Viking Press, 1971. 251p.

A homefront story about three patriotic young children who collect tin foil and scrap rubber and grow a Victory garden in a small midwestern town in the 1940s. The boy, Joe, also wants to trap enemy spies. Seemingly a game at first, the three come to believe they have really discovered foreign agents in the person of a local spinster and her boy friend. It all turns out to be a case of black marketeering rendered with suitable suspense for young people.

J285   Taylor, Theodore. *The Children's War*. Garden City, N.Y.: Doubleday, 1971. 166p.

This juvenile story begins during the summer of 1941 on an imaginary Alaskan island. Twelve-year-old Dory is primarily interested in his gun, wolf pup, and hunting trips since his father, a Navy radio man, has been stationed on the island with Dory's mother. Dory tolerates school in spite of the new teacher who turns out to be a pacifist even after Pearl Harbor. The last half of the story takes place after the U.S. enters the war. The Japanese soon invade the island and imprison all of the men on a nearby island. When an Army commando turns up, Dory and his friend guide the soldier to the prison island. Although the prisoners are rescued, the commando and the teacher are killed. The narrative contrasts the idyllic prewar life of the young protagonist with the life and death reality of war.

J286   Uchida, Yoshiko. *Journey to Topaz: a story of the Japanese-American Evacuation.* New York: Scribner, 1971. 149p.

The central character is eleven-year-old Yuki in this obviously autobiographical novel about the relocation of Japanese-Americans on the West coast during the war. Her father is taken immediately into custody by the F.B.I. on the night of December 7, 1941 while the rest of the family, Yuki, her eighteen-year-old brother, and her mother, are sent to Topaz, the War Relocation Center in Utah. The bewilderment and sense of loss by the family and all the Japanese-Americans in general, are eloquently described by the author. The discomfort and deprivation of the camp is emotionally but incisively presented. Nonetheless, the internees attempt to live and behave as normally as possible while resolving to remain loyal to their country despite their bitter treatment by U.S. authorities. The narrative has a strong sense of authenticity all the more strengthened by the scattering of black-and-white drawings throughout the text.

J287   Wuorio, Eva-Lis. *Code: Polonaise.* New York: Rinehart and Winston, 1971. 198p.

This juvenile story begins in occupied Poland with a group of Polish children who have lost their families and now live in the ruins of Warsaw. Evading the German soldiers, the youngsters become an active contingent of the resistance movement. The children publish a clandestine newspaper for the Polish underground at great risk to themselves. When the Germans took over Poland they outlawed Chopin's music as a dangerous symbol of nationalism, but the young Poles respond by loudly singing the Military Polonaise whenever they can. This is a juvenile story that does not hesitate to deal forthrightly with the ghastly aspects of wartime atrocities in Poland.

1972

J288   Moskin, Marietta D. *I am Rosemarie*. New York: John Day,
        1972. 190p.

A fictional autobiography reminiscent of the diary of Anne
Frank. The novel relates the progressive impact of the German
invasion on Rosemarie Brenner and her family in Holland. She
describes her adolescent years from the time when she is
expelled from school and required to wear the yellow star, to
her progressive isolation from all of her former friends.
Eventually her family's home and possessions are confiscated
by the Nazis and all are sent to a concentration camp.
Rosemarie grows into womanhood during the five years
internment in the camps. This is a simple, straightforward
account of her experiences and survival.

J289   Rayner, Claire Berenice. *The Burning Summer*. London:
        Allison and Busby, 1972. 143p.

A view of the East End of London from the perspective of a
seven-year-old Jewish girl. She has been sent several times to
the countryside for her safety but she keeps running away to
return to London and her mother and baby brother. The
narrative consists of her impressions of the city during the
blitz. Ruthie loves her gas mask and reacts to the air raids and
bombs with naivete until she is partially buried with debris
during an air raid and slightly wounded. When her family is
bombed out, her mother at last decides to take them all to live
in the country and begin a new life away from the trauma of
the London raids.

J290   Reiss, Johanna. *The Upstairs Room*. New York: Thomas Y.
        Crowell, 1972. 196p.

An autobiographical novel based on the experiences of the
author. When the Germans occupy Holland they begin the
roundup of all Jews. The De Leeuw family is forced to split up
and the children, Annie and her older sister, are hidden for
several years in the bedroom of the farmhouse home of a
sympathetic Christian family. The reader soon has a good idea
of what it means never to leave the room or to see other
children (except only on your birthday), and the fear when
German soldiers are to be stationed in the farmhouse. The
characterizations are believable with the style in a direct,
almost documentary frankness. One thinks immediately of *The
Diary of a Young Girl* by Anne Frank.

J291   Zei, Alki. *Petros' War*. Translated from the Greek by Edward
       Fenton. London: Gollancz, 1972. 236p.; New York: Dutton,
       1972. 236p. [*Ho Megalos Peripatos tou Petrou*. Athens:
       Editions Kedros, 1971.]

This is the story of a ten-year-old boy called Petros and the
occupation of Greece at first by the Italians and then by the
Nazis. Although Petros works for the Greek resistance by
painting slogans on walls, his most dangerous mission is the
liberation of a dog from a German soldier. The general impact
of the novel is to describe the effects of the occupation on the
people of Athens--their suffering, the rationing, and all the
indignities of everyday life under the heel of a ruthless
conqueror. This is a juvenile story that paints a sympathetic
and highly realistic portrait of what life for the general
population in wartime Athens was really like.

1973

J292   Bawden, Nina. *Carrie's War*. London: Gollancz, 1973. 159p.;
       Philadelphia: Lippincott, 1973. 159p.

Nearly all of the narrative describes Carrie at the age of
twelve starting in 1939 when she and her little brother are
evacuated from London and taken to live in a small Welsh
mining town. They are lodged with a miserly old shopkeeper
and his unassertive sister. It is an austere and bleak life until
Carrie and her brother discover Druid's Bottom, the nearby
house of the shopkeeper's other sister who is a warm and
motherly woman. She tells the two children the story of the
"screaming skull" kept in the house and of the curse that hangs
over the house. This tale continues to fascinate Carrie and just
before she and her brother are due to leave permanently,
Carrie throws the skull into the adjacent pond. As the children
leave on the train early the next morning, Carrie is shocked to
see Druid's Bottom on fire. It is this image and her sense of
guilt for having caused the fire that has festered for nearly
thirty years when she returns to the town with her two
children.

J293   Fahrmann, Willi. *The Year of the Wolves: The Story of an
       Exodus*. Translated by Stella Humphries. London: Oxford
       University Press, 1973. 195p. [*Das Jahr der Wolfe*.]

A sad refugee story placed in 1945 that depicts the horrors of
a civilian evacuation in East Prussia in the face of the Russian

breakthrough. The action focuses on the Bieumann family who increasingly confront the real possibility that they will never return to their home or perhaps even survive. Nevertheless, the emphasis is on family solidarity in the face of adversity regardless of what the future brings.

J294   Greene, Bette. *Summer of My German Soldier*. New York: Dial Press, 1973. 230p.

This is primarily a story of young adolescence, self-search, and family rejection. The narrator and protagonist is Patty Bergen, a twelve-year-old Jewish girl who is a rejected daughter and in her search for friendship and love befriends Anton, a young German POW, when he visits her father's store. After he escapes she hides him. Although Patty is Jewish, this issue is never discussed. Rather, the coming of age of Patty is seen through a melodramatic prism and the plot slides over one cliche after another concluding with her stay in a girl's reformatory for her aid and comfort to an enemy.

J295   Procházka, Jan. *Long Live the Republic (All About Me, and Julie, and the End of the Great War)*. Translated from the Czechoslovakian by Peter Kussi. Garden City, N.Y.: Doubleday, 1973. 243p. [*At' Zije Republika (Já a Julina a K'onec Velke Války)*. Praha: Státni Nakl. Détské Knihy, 1966. 175p.]

Describes Olda, a twelve-year-old boy, and his family's valuable possession, a beautiful horse. The war is constantly a threat hanging over the boy. Three German soldiers who retreat through the village as the Russians advance, steal the horse. After the theft, Olda resolves to steal horses from the Cossacks. This is a picaresque and comic tale, but also shocking, as the sensitive Olda watches the leaders of the village turn scavengers, and sees his best friend hanged as a collaborator. The story is based on the personal experiences of the author when the Russians drove out the German Army in 1945.

J296   Sachs, Marilyn. *A Pocket Full of Seeds*. Garden City, N.Y.: Doubleday, 1973. 137p.

This story is told from the perspective of an eight-year-old Jewish girl, Nicole Nieman, who lives in France at the time of the German occupation. The time period is from May of 1938 to February 1944. She describes the growing and pervasive Nazi terror as it extends across Europe and gradually embraces her own home town and family. When her parents are taken away Nicole begins to live with the constant possibility that she may never see them again as well as the thought that she may also be taken away. This is a poignant juvenile novel based on the actual childhood experiences of a friend of the author.

J297   Suhl, Yuri. *Uncle Misha's Partisans*. New York: Four Winds Press, 1973. 211p.

Motele, a twelve-year-old whose Jewish parents have been murdered, has just managed to stay alive by picking up coins as he plays his violin, his only possession. Passing as a Ukrainian gentile, Motele is now safe with his own people, the famous group of Jews known as "Uncle Misha's" partisans. He takes care of the supplies and horses of these freedom fighters, who hide deep in the forest and strike at the Germans whenever possible, and then quickly disappear. Motele gets his opportunity to be a partisan, when his violin wins him employment in the German regional command headquarters. There he entertains the officers with music, and relates information to "Uncle Misha," the leader of the partisans. He is also able to infiltrate a town that is a German stronghold, and plant explosives in an unused room in the Officers' House, which kill its occupants. The novel depicts Jews as fighters, instead of concentration-camp victims, and is based on the lives of actual resistance fighters.

J298   Welch, June Rayfield. *Dave's Tune*. Dallas: G.L.A. Press, 1973. 207p.

The jacket of this juvenile tale calls this a novel of Texas in the summer of 1944. The protagonist is a typical sixteen-year-old who is mostly concerned with his job, girls, and his older brother who is a pilot of a B-17. The major theme is the act of growing up during the war years. This is the time of scrap drives, sugar and gas rationing, and Victory gardens.

J299   Wuorio, Eva-Lis. *To Fight in Silence*. New York: Holt, Rinehart and Winston, 1973. 216p.

The story chronicles the struggle of the resistance in Denmark and in Norway against their Nazi conquerors during the early years of the war. The plot focuses on the family of Danish patriot Axel Jensen. Two of the children and their families live in Denmark and Norway. One daughter, married to a prominent Jewish pianist in Germany, escapes to Denmark with her two young children. One of the proudest moments in the Danish chronicle of the war is incorporated in the story: the successful efforts of the Danes to evacuate more than 8,000 Danish Jews to safety in Sweden. The factual background of events in this novel have been thoroughly researched and have been smoothly woven into a dramatic narrative.

1974

J300   Benchley, Nathaniel. *Bright Candles: A Novel of the Danish Resistance*. New York: Harper and Row, 1974. 256p.

This story of Danish resistance begins as the German takeover commences. The protagonist, Jens Hansen, is a sixteen-year-old in Copenhagen whose indignation about the German occupation inspires him and his friend Ole to carry out simple tactics against the Germans. At first the boys scrawl graffiti on walls of the enemy headquarters, and pour sugar in the gas tanks of Nazi staff cars. In time Jens becomes an expert with the older resistance saboteurs. His father is arrested, his mother disappears, and Ole is killed. Then Jens is captured and imprisoned, but in time an Allied bombing attack on the prison releases him, and he stays in hiding until the end of the war.

J301   Burch, Robert. *Hut School and the Wartime Home-front Heroes*. New York: Viking Press, 1974. 140p.

The slight plot of this homefront juvenile story describes the reactions of Kate and her sixth-grade school mates in a small Georgia town. The children are forced to leave their school building and use an old cabin until the new classrooms are built. They accept this change along with all the war related hardships such as food shortages, rationing, and separation from their fathers and brothers, etc. as a matter of course even when their favorite teacher joins the WAVES. The setting nostalgically evokes rural Georgia about 1943.

J302   Evenhuis, Gertie. *What About Me?* Translated from the Dutch by Lance Salway. Harmondsworth: Longman Young Books, 1974. 95p. [*En Waarom Ik Niet?* Amsterdam: Deltos Elsevier, 1970.]

A juvenile story placed in German-occupied Amsterdam in 1943. The hero is eleven-year-old Dirk Waterman who inadvertently becomes involved in the Dutch resistance after being turned down by his older brother because Dirk is too young. A brief but accurate view not only of the grim life in the occupied city but also an account of Dutch resistance activities and Gestapo repression.

J303 Streatfeild, Noel. *When the Siren Wailed*. London: Collins, 1974. 157p. [Title in U.S.: *When the Sirens Wailed*. New York: Random House, 1976. 176p.]

A juvenile story about the wartime evacuation of children from London to safe areas in the countryside. The plot deals with three poor south London children who are sent to Dorset under the care of an upright country squire. This results in a clash of cultural backgrounds but a mutual respect of a sort is maintained by both the squire and the children. The death of the squire causes the children to run away back to London only to find their home destroyed and their mother in a hospital. The story ends on an up-beat note when all of the family are reunited in the country.

J304 Volstad, Edith. *Again I See the Mountains*. Los Angeles: Volstad, 1974. 152p.

The plot focuses on a small Norwegian island village under the German occupation. The narrative describes the hardships and deprivations suffered by the inhabitants, including those Norwegian patriots killed in the struggle. Chief among the characters is Katherine Viken, the youngest member of the local resistance, who spends her teen-age years working against the Germans. The story is autobiographical for the author lived in Norway, and was arrested by the Gestapo at the age of fifteen; thus receiving first-hand experience of the "judicial system of tyrants."

J305 Woodford, Peggy. *Backwater War*. London: Bodley Head, 1974. 188p.

A chronicle of the lives of the Guernsey Islanders during the 1940-1943 years under the German occupation. The narrative specifically deals with the family of Anna Hardy who is seventeen as the story begins. The family problems are compounded when they protect a young Polish political prisoner who has escaped from a nearby German prison camp, and help him try to reach England. The Hardy family life is one of privation and depression as they share their meager rations with one another and grow to resent bitterly the German occupation of their land.

1975

J306   Brancato, Robin F. *Don't Sit under the Apple Tree*. New York:
       Knopf, 1975. 163p.

       A juvenile story set during the summer of 1945 and featuring
       a young adolescent tomboy who serves as the first person
       narrator on life in a small Pennsylvania town. The impact of
       the war on the lives of her friends is illustrated through the
       deaths of brothers and fathers during the closing months of the
       war. The primary focus is on the coming of age of Ellis
       Carpenter with the impact of the war on the homefront as a
       secondary theme.

J307   Johnson, Gertrude F. *A Gathering of Lambs: A Story From
       World War II*. St. Louis: Concordia Publishing House, 1975.
       144p.

       Describes the experiences of a German family living in a
       German community in eastern Poland. The daughter is ten
       years old when the war begins, and her Polish classmates start
       to taunt her and her Jewish friends. With the German
       occupation, the Nazi indoctrination begins, and the family is
       forced to simulate agreement. The effects of German cruelty
       upon both Jews and Poles alike becomes apparent to the young
       girl. Her family smuggles food into the Jewish ghetto until they
       are ordered to move into the Polish Corridor. When the
       German forces retreat westward, the Germans living in Poland
       are also ordered westward, but the family is able to escape into
       the British zone and safety. The narrative is based on the
       wartime experiences of the author.

J308   Kerr, Judith. *The Other Way Round*. London: Collins, 1975.
       256p.; New York: Coward-McCann and Geoghegan, 1975.
       256p.

       Describes a German family's adaptation to life in London
       during the blitz when refugee families are frequently without
       work and subject to English resentment and suspicion. Their
       Jewish ancestry and the father's political writings have forced
       them to leave Germany. Anna, the daughter, finds work as a
       secretary, and develops as a creative artist. Her brother is
       enrolled at Cambridge, but is determined to join the RAF
       which he is eventually permitted to do in spite of being
       classified as an enemy alien. This is the sequel to *When Hitler
       Stole Pink Rabbit* (see item J283).

J309 Nöstlinger, Christine. *Fly Away Home*. Translated from the German by Anthea Bell. New York: Franklin Watts, 1975. 134p. [*Maikäfer, Flieg! Mein Vater, Das Kriegsende, Cohn und Ich*. Weinheim, Basel: Beltz und Gelberg, 1973. 175p.]

Based on the childhood experiences of the author, this juvenile story concerns an eight-year-old girl, Christel Goth, who is living in Vienna at the end of the war when the German military regime is replaced by the Soviet combat forces. She is aware that her father must stay hidden, for he is a deserter hiding out from the German Army and she fears that the approaching Russians will view him only as an enemy soldier. All the same, the family is lucky to be together with even a little food, which Christel has found after searching an abandoned house. When their home in a poor Vienna section is bombed, the destitute family takes refuge outside the city with friends only to undergo further hardships. This is a sensit story that portrays the ordinariness of daily life, even under terrible conditions.

J310 Paul, Leslie [Allen]. *The Waters and the Wild*. London: Cassell, 1975. 181p.; New York: St. Martin's Press, 1975. 181p.

The war is far distant in this nostalgic reminiscence about growing up in East Anglia, England. The estate of the local earl is now an army battle school with nightly exercises using fireworks which provide a passing distraction for the local children. Two boys: Harry, who is eleven, and Ben, a year younger, find a secret hideout during the winter on a lake island on the earl's estate. They build a raft and fish for a gigantic pike. The text uses ample examples of the local dialect to describe the boys' experiences as their hideaway is taken over by the local troops.

J311 Suhl, Yuri. *On the Other Side of the Gate. A Novel*. New York: Franklin Watts, 1975. 149p.

Inspired by a true episode, the story describes life in occupied Poland during the war, especially that of the Jews. A Jewish couple, Hershel and Lena Bregman, are confined to the Warsaw ghetto. Since the Nazis have outlawed pregnancies in the ghetto, the Bregmans are forced to deliver their child secretly. Only close relatives and a few trusted members of the ghetto underground are aware that there is a baby boy in the ghetto. When the Jews are to be deported, a sympathetic local Polish architect helps to smuggle out the eighteen-month-old child and adopts him. This is a holocaust novel that captures the suspense and tension of the desperate effort of the Jews to survive and save their offspring.

J312   Terlouw, Jan. *Winter in Wartime*. Glasgow: Blackie, 1975. 160p. [*Oorlogswinter*. Rotterdam: Lemniscaat, 1972. 164p.]

A story about the German occupation of Holland and the Dutch resistance movement. The central character is fifteen-year-old Michiel who suddenly has the sole responsibility for the care of an injured English paratrooper. When his father and nine others are taken hostage and shot, Michiel suddenly is disabused of any romantic notions about war and its consequences. Based on the author's own experiences, the plot realistically recreates the bitter conditions of the occupation of Holland. This book won the award for the Best Dutch Juvenile Book for 1973.

J313   Van Stockum, Hilda. *The Borrowed House*. New York: Farrar, Straus and Giroux, 1975. 215p.

Janna, a twelve-year-old girl, moves into an Amsterdam house "borrowed" for her mother and father who are actors. Her parents have come from Berlin to perform for the German occupation forces, and the Dutch family of van Arkels are evicted to provide a place for them. Mementos in the house, clothing for a girl about her age, and the many mysteries of a Jewish household raise her curiosity, and she discovers that her knowledge of Dutch life is at odds with what she has learned in her Hitler Youth Movement training. She comes to recognize the meaning of the German occupation and the fate of the Jews, and develops her own view of the realities of life about her. This is an unusual story of wartime Holland from a German point of view.

J314   Westall, Robert. *The Machine-gunners*. London: Macmillan, 1975. 189p.

A tough but sensitive juvenile story based on a similar incident which occurred in the Netherlands. The protagonist is Chas McGill, an English teenager living in Garmouth during 1941. The region is subjected to daily German air raids. Chas finds a crashed enemy bomber in a wood near the town. The machine gun is still intact and Chas and his friends dismantle the weapon and build a secret emplacement so as to use the gun against the feared and hated German bombers. The authorities are only able to locate the machine gun when the boys finally shoot it when they mistake some local Polish troops for the invading Germans. In the confusion, they shoot their only captured German soldier who has become their friend. This is a relatively involved narrative filled with irony and insight into human nature. The story won the 1976 Carnegie Medal.

1976

J315 Benchley, Nathaniel. *A Necessary End: A Novel of World War II*. New York: Harper and Row, 1976. 193p.

A juvenile novel written in diary form by seventeen-year-old Ralph Bowers who joined the Navy before he was drafted because life was so dull in New England. His account contains plenty of naval technical details. He serves as a signalman on an Atlantic coast patrol and convoy vessel and describes the boredom of non-combat duty at sea. After the end of the war in Europe his ship is sent through the Canal to the Pacific theater where he serves at Guam, Okinawa and the Philippine areas until the Japanese surrender. The diary tends to be a reportorial account of all the mundane and prosaic happenings aboard ship interlarded with news reports on the progress of the war both in Europe and the Far East.

J316 Corcoran, Barbara. *Axe-time, Sword-time*. New York: Atheneum, 1976. 204p.

Recounts the struggle of eighteen-year-old Elinor Golden, who was slightly brain-damaged when she was struck by a golf ball as a child. Even when her brother and her boyfriend join the service, Elinor considers that she has little time to worry about the war. Her father's friend, a German war refugee, helps her overcome her concern about her mental situation. To achieve independence and maturity, Elinor finds her niche by doing defense work.

J317 Forman, James [Douglas]. *The Survivor*. New York: Farrar, Straus and Giroux, 1976. 272p.

Describes a Jewish family in the Netherlands during the war as they one by one fall victim to the Nazi terror. The two twin sons ignore their brother Daniel's warning of Hitler's plan toward the Jews in Holland. When the Germans invade, Daniel joins the Dutch underground and succeeds in hiding some of his family for a time. Eventually, however, only one of the twins is the sole survivor of the family. The grandmother dies of shock and old age; the grandfather kills himself; the mother dies from exposure; while the father and oldest daughter perish in Auschwitz. Eventually, David the surviving twin, returns to Amsterdam when the war is over. The horrors of the holocaust are presented dramatically through the grim and realistic narrative and its focus on the members of one family.

J318   Garrigue, Sheila. *All the Childlren Were Sent Away, A Novel.* Scarsdale, New York: Bradbury Press, 1976. 171p.

This is a sensitive and well written juvenile story about the evacuation of children from England early in the war. Sara Warren, just eight years old, is sent with a shipload of other English children to live with relatives in Canada. The sea journey takes place during June and July of 1940 at the height of the German air raids and U-boat threat. Most of the narrative describes the experiences of Sara on shipboard, her new found friends, Maggie and Ernie, and her gruff guardian, Lady Drume. The boat is attacked by a German sub and nearly sunk. This and the other experiences of the crossing to Newfoundland are seen through the eyes of Sara who lives the war years with her aunt and uncle in Vancouver, B.C.

J319   Hickman, Janet. *The Stones*. New York: Macmillan, 1976. 116p.

This is a juvenile story placed against the backdrop of the war. An old man with a German name becomes harassed by a group of little boys in a small town in the Midwest. When the reclusive old man in frustration shoots off his shotgun in response to their pranks, parents become alarmed. But one of the boys comes to see the old man in human terms which places him at odds with his mischievous friends. This is a low-key and thoughtful tale of the consequences of behavior which has only an incidental relationship to the war.

J320   Lustig, Arnost. *Darkness Casts No Shadow*. Washington: Inscape, 1976. 144p.

This is a short novel based on the personal experiences of the author. The setting is the Terezin "model" concentration camp outside Prague. Czech Jews are there waiting to be selected for the final camps in Germany. Two boys are able to escape from a German transport train when it is strafed by an American aircraft. The boys hide in the nearby dense forest, constantly battling cold and hunger while heading back to their home in Prague. The narrative intermittantly has flashbacks to the other camps and ghettos where human brutality was commonplace: death by exposure and starvation; orphaned children with only the memory of their murdered parents; and the sexual perversion of the camp guards. The quiet prose style seems to reveal better the actual horror of what actually happened through the effect on the mental state of the children who had to watch their parents taken to the crematoriums. The sparse and understated narrative leaves with the reader the nagging realization that this fiction really isn't fiction.

1977

J321   Burnford, Sheila [Every]. *Bel Ria*. Toronto: McClelland and Stewart, 1977. 203p.; Boston: Little, Brown, 1977. 215p.

A sentimental story about the wanderings of a small performing dog in France, at sea, and in England during the war. The tale begins in the summer of 1940 on the refugee-clogged roads of western France. The Gypsy woman mistress of the dog is killed during a Stuka attack. The dog is successively adopted by various humans and at one point even has a monkey for a companion. Intelligent and with a spunky charm, the dog seems to exercise a remarkable and positive effect on everyone it meets as the dog journeys through the war-torn landscape on the retreat across France, evacuation by a boat and its sinking, the bombing of Plymouth, etc. and the final haven of the dog in a peaceful home in England. This is a story for children. A major theme is the rapport and interaction between humans and animals.

J322   Dank, Milton. *The Dangerous Game*. Philadelphia: Lippincott, 1977. 157p.

The story covers the day-to-day activities of the French Resistance. Charles, the fifteen-year-old son of a French father and an American mother, is left to fend for himself when the Germans occupy Paris in 1940. He joins the local Resistance and is nearly killed by the Gestapo on his first mission. The narrative seems to pull no punches in describing the details of the deadly serious and frequently tragic life of a Resistance fighter. There is a dash of romance for Charles. By the conclusion of the story he find himself in England in 1943, ready and eager to join up with the Free French intelligence service. The author has based much of his fictional narrative on his earlier history of the French Resistance published in

1974. The novel is a thriller with most of the attention on the action rather than on character development or writing style.

J323   Frederick, Lee. *Crash Dive*. Belmont, CA: Fearon-Pitman, 1977. 59p.

Describes a new kind of German submarine and one of the first American destroyers equipped with sonar. Commander Rohmer, one of the best German Navy U-boat commanders, is placed in charge of the new sub. He is ordered to proceed to Portsmouth, England and try to maneuver through the mine nets and torpedo vessels in the harbor. Captain Coffey directs his American destroyer to attack the sub. What ensues is a duel between the destroyer and the sub involving torpedoes, depth charges, and all the rest of the available weaponry and techniques. Eventually, the destroyer tricks the sub to the surface and sinks the U-boat after rescuing Rohmer and his crew. The narrative follows the battle from the point of view of both commanders and demonstrates how important deception can be in sea battles.

J324   Levoy, Myron. *Alan and Naomi*. New York: Harper and Row, 1977. 192p.

The action begins in New York City in 1944. Alan, a young Jewish boy obsessed by his games of stickball after school, is persuaded by his parents to spend his afternoons socializing with Naomi, a refugee girl from France. Her father had been murdered in front of her by the Gestapo and she has since withdrawn from nearly every human activity. Although Alan at first resents his loss of play time, he soon sees that his presence has helped Naomi come out of her withdrawn state. Unfortunately, an act of vicious prejudice by a school student sends Naomi off again into the depths of fear and withdrawal. Alan fights the ignoramous and rushes off in search of the missing Naomi, eventually to find that her condition has so worsened that she now must be hospitalized. Ethnic and religious prejudice are especially well illustrated in the poignant and heart-wrenching conclusion.

J325   Rice, Earle, Jr. *Tiger, Lion, Hawk; A Story of the Flying Tigers*. Belmont, CA: Fearon-Pitman, 1977. 60p.

Drew Elsmore is the pilot-hero of this exceedingly brief fictionalized account of Flying Tiger air combat against the Japanese. The action is focused on the period from December 23, 1941 to the early spring of 1942. A documentary slice-of-life account about this famous World War II group, it could only have been intended for juveniles since it cannot be taken seriously as fiction.

J326   Rose, Anne [K.]. *Refugee*. New York: Dial Press, 1977. 118p.

This story follows Elke Colbert, a twelve-year-old Belgian Jewish girl through the war years in Antwerp and later in New York. The narrative is based on Elke's diary and from letters written by her and to her from her friends after she leaves Antwerp for New York City. The censured letters hint of the horrors suffered by her friends and relatives who had escaped to Rio de Janeiro a few days before enemy troops entered Belgium. The story describes Elke's adaptation to American life, her difficulties in new surroundings, her concern about friends still trapped in Europe, and her pain when learning of news of deaths at home. This is an autobiographical story.

J327   Standen, Michael. *Over the Wet Lawn*. Oxford, England: Oxford University Press, 1977. 174p.

A juvenile adventure story placed in England during the first year or so of the war. Four children decide to unravel the mystery of what they believe is a spy ring. The writing is not felicitous--the style tends to be stilted and awkward. The title is taken from a poem of Siegried Sassoon.

1978

J328   Anderson, Margaret J. *Searching for Shona*. New York: Knopf, 1978. 159p.

The narrative is based on the evacuation of children from Edinburgh at the beginning of the war. Two girls, preferring each other's destination, decide to trade places, names, and lives. Marjorie is a shy girl from a wealthy family who takes the name of Shona McInnes, an orphan bound for southern Scotland. Neither girl realizes that the war will last nearly six years and result in far greater changes in their lives than ever anticipated. The major thrust of the story is the search for identity by Marjorie. This is a somewhat unusual juvenile story in which the war is a distant backdrop.

J329   Bloch, Maria Halun. *Displaced Person*. New York: Lothrop, Lee and Shepard, 1978. 191p.

The general theme is the lot of the displaced person during the last weeks of the war. The protagonist is fourteen-year-old Stefan from the Ukraine who with his father has fled from the Russians along with large numbers of other refugees. Stefan and his father settle temporarily in a German refugee camp and make a number of new friends but soon move on as a result of the bombing and strafing by Allied aircraft. While everyone is hoping for the Americans to arrive, they still wonder whether they will be any better than the Nazis or the Soviets. Stefan's father is killed in an American strafing attack and the boy is now truly alone. The prospect of freedom from the political constraints of the Soviets and the Germans tends to terrify Stefan at first but he is forced by circumstance and his father's death to recognize that it is just as important as any security. Stefan is pictured as an individual who is a victim of historical circumstances but is able to survive and endure because of his character. The narrative presents a realistic study of the fate of refugees in Germany before, during, and after the advance of American troops, and the postwar partition of Germany into various zones by the big powers.

J330   Fife, Dale. *North of Danger*. New York: Dutton, 1978. 72p.

The time is 1940 and a twelve-year-old Norwegian boy makes a 200 mile trek by skis to warn his scientist father not to return to their village near Spitsbergen. The British have evacuated the village in anticipation of an immediate German invasion from the sea. His father is a likely resistance suspect and would doubtless be imprisoned or shot by the Nazis. Barely surviving the ice and snow storms, the young boy encounters a helpful trapper who volunteers to guide the boy to his father. Part of the suspense is whether the trapper might be a German agent in disguise. He isn't. They reach and warn the father and all ends well. Supposedly, the story is based on an actual incident from the war.

J331   Griese, Arnold A.. *The Wind Is Not a River*. New York: Thomas Y. Crowell, 1978. 108p.

This juvenile story takes place on the island of Attu, off the Alaskan coast in June of 1942. Japanese soldiers have arrived to occupy the island where 47 Aleuts live in their village. Two youngsters, Susan and her younger brother, escape the Japanese, but helplessly watch the capture of their village. Hiding out in the hills, the children discover a wounded Japanese soldier. They face a dilemma when they recognize that the young Japanese soldier will die without their help, but the soldier will interfere with their plan to take a boat to Kiska and tell the United States military of the invasion. However, the soldier offers a bargain: his freedom for theirs. The theme is how humanitarian ethics are rewarded when a moral choice is made.

J332 Rees, David. *The Exeter Blitz*. London: Hamish Hamilton, 1978. 116p.; New York: Elsevier/Nelson Books, 1978. 128p.

This juvenile story attempts to recreate the feeling and experiences of a family living through an air raid. Exeter is described during a raid in the evening and on a morning in May of 1942. The Lockwood family is separated during the raid. The father and younger daughter are at home while the mother is at a dress shop; the older daughter is at the cinema; and the adolescent son watches the action from the local cathedral tower. After the all clear, each of the Lockwoods provide their individual impression of the raid which results in an unusual composite picture of how several people observe and react to the same air raid.

1979

J333 Allan, Mabel Esther. *Tomorrow is a Lovely Day*. London: Abelard-Schuman, 1979. 128p. [Title in U.S.: *A Lovely Tomorrow*. New York: Dodd, Mead, 1980. 190p.]

A homefront juvenile story that traces the experiences and adjustments of a fifteen-year-old girl from New Year's Eve in 1941 when a V2 rocket kills her parents until the autumn of 1945 when she is able to return to London, her home before the traumatic loss of her mother and father. In the intervening period she is taken to live with her aunt in the country. Although the war is ever present in the background (whether the Normandy invasion or the atomic bomb drop on Japan) this is primarily a tale of her adjustment to life as an orphan and to the people and circumstances of life around her in England.

J334 Donaldson, Margaret [C.]. *Journey Into War*. London: André Deutsch, 1979. 152p.

During the summer of Dunkirk, three children who have been stranded in wartime France, organize their own resistance to the Germans. Janey, a ten-year-old English girl on her way to England decides to make her way north and find her father who is supposed to be in St. Quentin. When she gets there her father is gone, and she finds the town in German hands. She meets two stranded Polish boys of her age, who rescue her when she falls in the hands of the Gestapo. A typical juvenile novel in most respects, this story has a Gestapo character who shows some sensitivity for a little lost girl.

J335   Gessner, Lynne. *Edge of Darkness*. New York: Walker, 1979. 181p.

This is a story about Latvia between June 1941 and October 1944. After the German Army forces the Russians out of Latvia, David Ozol, a thirteen-year-old farm boy, and his family rejoice in being free of the horrible NKVD. But the German occupation is no improvement. David is tortured by the Soviet secret police in an attempt to get him to betray his father. He refuses, but all the same believes he has betrayed his father. Instead, his godfather turns out to be the traitor. This is an almost unbelievable story of terrorist tactics in a country swept three times by war and twice by the Russians.

J336   Mace, Elisabeth. *Brother Enemy*. London: Deutsch, 1979. 138p.

This juvenile tale begins in 1937 with Andreas, the Jewish nine-year-old protagonist, who is sent to England for his safety. Most of the story (pages 24-255) covers the war years and describes the experiences of Andreas with one foster family after another while in English schools. He sustains himself with the hope that after the war he can return home to Hamburg to find his family. Most of the narrative recounts his associations with his school mates and their varied (and sometimes cruel) response to a foreign boy from Germany. After the war he does return home only to find that England is now his true home. This is a short and sensitive story about how a young German refugee is received and accepted in wartime England.

J337   Mazer, Harry. *The Last Mission, A Novel*. New York: Delacorte Press, 1979. 182p.

The adolescent hero is Jack Raab who at the age of fifteen lies his way into the Army Air Force where he eventually is assigned to combat duty in England. All goes well for him and his fellow crew members until the 25th mission when the bomber is hit and Jack bails out to be the only survivor. He lands in Germany and ends up in a POW camp but is liberated home when Germany is defeated. The narrative is related in a quick-action journalistic style interspersed with typical G.I. language. Not only is this an emotionally moving account but also a convincing portrayal of Jack's misgivings as a Jew on German soil and his growing but believable misgivings about the stupidity of war.

J338 Rice, Earle, Jr. *The Animals.* Belmont, CA: Fearon-Pitman, 1979. 58p.

Captain Clay Denison of the U.S. Army Air Force is on his thirteenth mission into Germany in his B-17. His bomber is shot down and he is captured by Germans who take him to a German air force hospital in France. While Denison is recuperating, a French nurse called "Porcupine" (a secret member of the French Resistance Alliance of Animals which uses animal code names) arranges for his escape from the hospital. Denison learns that the German pilots are planning to fly to Heaslip Field, where Winston Churchill is living, and kill him. He then manages to cross the English Channel and inform the British who prepare to destroy the German planes as they arrive. This is a typical juvenile war story.

J339 Sallis, Susan. *A Time for Everything.* New York: Harper and Row, 1979. 218p.

Set in a small village in Gloucestershire, England, this narrative views the war through the eyes of Lily Freeman, a young country girl. She is eleven when her father is inducted into the army. Events force Lily into an early maturity as she faces the many problems caused by the war and the absence of her father. She must also cope with the slyness of the twelve-year-old London evacuee who is staying with her family. The characterization and conversations appear to realistically capture the behavior of Lily and her age group.

J340 Tsuchiya, Yukio. *Poor Elephants: A Sad Story of Animals and People and War.* Tokyo: Kin-no-Hoshi-Sha, 1979. c1970. 31p. [Title in U.S.: *Faithful Elephants: True Story of Animals, People, and War.* Translated by Tomoko Tsuchiya Dykes. Boston: Houghton Mifflin, 1988. 32p.] [*Kawaiso Na Zo.* Tokyo: 1979.]

An unusual juvenile story about the effect of the war in Japan. A Tokyo zoo keeper narrates the tale of how there came to be graves at the zoo. When Tokyo was hit repeatedly by bombs the authorities feared that the zoo might be destroyed

and the animals released to cause havoc in the city. Hence, all
of the zoo animals were to be killed. Only the elephants
refused to eat their poisoned food and had hides too tough for
the poison syringes to penetrate. Thus they had to be starved to
death, a slow and agonizing process for the animals and their
keepers. Very likely this will be a disturbing story for both
adults and children. The underlying theme is the nature of
death and dying and even how a few can be sacrificed for the
good of all.

J341   Westall, Robert [Atkinson]. *Fathom Five*. London: Macmillan,
        1979. 242p.

It is 1943 in England as Charles McGill and his three friends
follow the clues which Charles claims are from the presence of
spies. They appear to indicate that a spy has been attempting to
communicate information from an Allied ship to German U-
boats. Their parents, the police, and other adults discourage the
four from continuing their search. But they persist, however,
and become involved in a mysterious murder. Nevertheless,
they prevent the bombing of an English ship. In time Charles
realizes that war is really not a game. Although the story
becomes unduly complex at times, it seems realistic and largely
convincing. The dialogue is flavored with the local English
speech idioms. This is the sequel to *The Machine Gunners*
(item J314).

1980

J342   Donaldson, Margaret [C.]. *The Moon's on Fire*. London:
        Deutsch, 1980. 138p.

This story begins in London in September of 1940 when the
Germans were thought to be preparing to invade England. The
plot involves three children, a girl and her two Polish friends
who have recently escaped from Europe. The Polish boys have
traveled through Yugoslavia, then hid on a ship bound for
Marseilles, travelled north through France, and then eluded the
Germans on a fishing boat that took them to England. The
boys, however, become unhappy with their London sponsor,
leave the home and attempt to join either the Polish Army unit
in London or the Polish air squadron. Neither will accept the
boys due to their young age. The boys then experience several
London bomb attacks and become well acquainted with London
air raid sirens, civil defense wardens, and with the
underground tube as a bomb shelter. The narrative makes a

special effort to show the disastrous consequences of the German air blitz on London. Each chapter is labeled with a month, day, and year, and significant events of the war on these dates are carefully explained for young readers.

J343 Lingard, Joan. *The File on Fraulein Berg*. New York: Elsevier/Nelson Books, 1980. 153p.

Set in Belfast and Dublin, the story describes the persecution of a German substitute language teacher by three Belfast fourth-form schoolgirls under the mistaken belief that the teacher is an enemy spy. The girls follow Fraulein Berg's comings and goings around Belfast. When all three girls go on an excursion into Dublin, in a neutral country, they find that their teacher has taken the same train there. This seems evidence of her traitorous intent. The story illuminates the manner in which wartime can distort thinking, and makes the revelation of the teacher's Jewishness all the more striking. The other emphasis is on the lives of civilians during wartime: blackouts, queueing, shortages, rationing, curtailed shopping and goods, etc.

J344 Lowry, Lois. *Autumn Street*. Boston: Houghton Mifflin, 1980. 188p.

Elizabeth, the first-person narrator, nostalgically introduces her family story during the war years. When her father leaves for the Pacific war, she, her older sister and her pregnant mother leave New York to live with her grandparents in Pennsylvania on a street called Autumn Street. Elizabeth is only six at the time. She forms a special relationship with Tatie, the black housekeeper-cook, and Charley, her street-wise son. This is mainly a story about growing up, of separation, and of human relationships largely viewed from an adult perspective masquerading as a six and seven-year-old girl. Autumn Street comes to symbolize this precious stage of life for Elizabeth and its conclusion when her father returns home from the war minus a leg.

J345 Pelgrom, Els. *The Winter When Time was Frozen*. Translated from the Dutch by Maryka and Raphael Rudnik. New York: Morrow, 1980. 253p. [*De Kinderen Van Het Achtste Woud*. Amsterdam: Uitgeverij Kosmos, 1977. 204p.]

After the battle of Arnhem, twelve-year-old Noortje and her father are forced to flee from their home and find refuge with the humane Everingen family at Klaphek Farm. But the war seems omnipresent. Even when the Allies are able to advance, the Germans still attempt to hold on. Although most people are hungry, Noortje and her father are fortunate to have found shelter with a farm family who courageously give sanctuary to those in need. This is a simple tale about how a twelve-year-old girl moves from childhood to maturity under adverse and unusual circumstances.

J346 Picchio, Carlo. *Freedom Fighter*. Translated by Isabel Quigly. Oxford; New York: Oxford University Press, 1980. 140p. [*Scarola.*]

This juvenile story is placed during the German occupation of Italy (1943-1945). The hero is a twelve-year-old orphan boy who joins a local Italian partisan group. Due to his age, he is able to perform various tasks of sabotage without the Nazis suspecting him. This is not a romantic view of war but rather a realistic portrait that should impress young readers with the seriousness of wartime.

1981

J347 Aaron, Chester. *Gideon, A Novel*. New York: Lippincott Junior Books: distributed by Harper, 1981. 192p.

This is a powerful holocaust juvenile novel based on the composite actual experiences of a number of Jewish survivors. Although the story is presumably directed at juveniles, the incidents and explicit atrocity details are relatively strong stuff even for adults. Gideon is the central character and is followed through his Warsaw ghetto experiences as he risks his life to sneak food into the ghetto for the starving inmates. He finally escapes with a small group of Aryan juvenile thieves and fights with the Polish resistance but is caught and sent to Treblinka. He later becomes involved in a rebellion at the camp and is able to escape. The descriptions are blunt and brutal. There is no pussy-footing by the author in showing the incredible inhumanity of the Germans and others twisted by the war. This is a strong documentary slice of life.

J348 Allan, Mabel Esther. *A Strange Enchantment*. London: Abelard-Schuman, 1981. 128p.

This story begins in 1939 and coincides with the first year of the war. The principal character is a sixteen-year-old girl who pretends she is a year older and volunteers for the British

Women's Land Army, an organization devoted to war work across the English countryside. She is sent to an agricultural college for training before going to work on a farm as her war contribution. The plot is a well worn formula approach that emphasizes the daily details of farm work. The war itself seems very distant and has little direct impact on the daily lives of the characters. But the story does convey the fervor with which the English volunteered to work for the good of the country. It is not difficult to believe that this novel will only appeal to young girls.

J349 Durrant, George D. *There's an Enemy Sub in Potter's Pond.* Salt Lake City: Bookcraft, 1981. 74p.

The juvenile protagonist, Jake, learns about the meaning of friendship, courage, and loyalty when the Japanese attack Pearl Harbor and public opinion in his neighborhood threatens his friendship with his young Japanese friend. Not seen.

J350 Fife, Dale. *Destination Unknown.* New York: Dutton, 1981. 96p.

The war has stranded Jon Lunde and his Norwegian fishing boat in the Faeroe Islands and his parents in England. So Jon hurriedly stows away aboard a boat bound for England, or so he thinks. Once underway, a crewman discovers Jon and puts him to work in the galley. When the crew learns that Norway has been occupied by the Germans, the boat is unable to return to Norway or to reach England. The crew then votes to head for America. After surviving storms, icebergs, and seasickness, they are stopped by a German U-boat, but when their skipper convinces the U-boat captain that they are only fishing, the vessel is permitted to continue and it eventually reaches the United States. The story is based on the wartime experience of a friend of the author.

J351 Hough, Richard Alexander. *Razor Eyes.* London: Dent, 1981. 128p.

This is the first-person narrative of Mick Boyd as he recollects his wartime experiences in the RAF. Along with his friend Bruno, he enlists at the age of eighteen on his birthday in 1940. He describes his pilot training, various missions, and his initial fears. The primary focus of the story is his solo mission to photograph and destroy an experimental German jet fighter at an airfield in France. The descriptions of his close calls and air evasions in order to protect his limited fuel supply and his precious photographs has conviction and drama. Mick just makes it back to crash-land on the Dover beach. Some libraries have classed this in juvenile fiction but it might just as appropriately appeal to adult readers.

J352   Magorian, Michelle. *Good Night, Mr. Tom*. London: Kestrel Books, Penguin Books, 1981. 304p.; New York: Harper and Row, 1981. 318p.

It is 1939 and the English village of Little Weirwold assumes an important role in the war effort. The village has been made to open its homes to slum children from the East End of London who have little or no experience with life in a country village. The story concentrates on nine-year-old Willie Beech who is housed with Thomas Oakley, a widower of sixty. In his new life, Willie learns that the town Grange has been converted into a convalescent military hospital and first-aid center. Actions such as fire watching, the call-up of the local young men for military service, and the first missing-in-action reports come to explain for Willie the reasons he was moved from the dangers of London. Thus, the boy from the slums becomes changed into a trusting and capable human being.

1982

J353   Campbell, Barbara. *A Girl Called Bob and a Horse Called Yoki*. New York: Dial Press, 1982. 167p.

Not seen.

J354   Elliott, Janice. *Secret Places*. New York: St. Martin's Press, 1982. 192p.

A juvenile tale about the effects of war on the students of Albert Lodge School for Girls, an English school near air-raid shelters and a POW camp housing German and Italian soldiers. Patience, an English girl, and Laura, a refugee from Germany, and new to the school, are the main characters. The families of both girls are separated due to the war. The father of Patience is on military duty in North Africa while the father of Laura is an anti-Nazi German scientist detained in England and forced to work on the atomic bomb. Laura as an outsider only has Patience as her friend. She serves as the scapegoat for the fears and frustrations of many of the other girls, and even some of the faculty. This is an impressionistic, sensitive, and witty view of adolescent emotions and schoolgirl attachments, especially during family separations caused by the impact of the war on England.

J355 Hartman, Evert. *War Without Friends*. Translated from the Dutch by Patricia Crampton. New York: Crown, 1982. 218p.; London: Chatto and Windus, 1982. 182p. [*Oorlog Zonder Vrienden.*]

Here is an unusual juvenile story about two and one-half years in the life of a teenager in German-occupied Holland from 1942 to 1944. Arnold Westervoort is the son of a low ranking Nazi official in the NSB, the Dutch equivalent of the Nazi party. Since Arnold is the only Nazi child in the school, he is constantly taunted and bullied. When a new boy arrives whose father is a high official in the party, Arnold logically turns in his direction for friendship. However, Arnold is no fool and now begins to see the fanaticism of the fascist movement, its evils, how it changes his father, tears at the structure of his family, and eventually destroys the family of the girl he likes. This is a low key narrative about the daily impact of National Socialism on the life of the young in Holland. Unfortunately, the story is poorly developed and the characterization rudimentary to be as commanding as it potentially should have been.

J356 Maruki, Toshi. *Hirochima No Pika*. New York: Lothrop, Lee and Shepard, 1982. unpaged [44p.] [*Hiroshima No Pika*. Tokyo: Komine Shoten, 1980.]

This is a powerful little story for juveniles and adults about the impact of the atomic bomb on Hiroshima. It is a mother's account of that horrible happening which causes her seven-year-old daughter's growth to be permanently arrested. The text is accompanied by a series of stunning illustrations painted by the author that powerfully reflect the instant desolation and radiation damage that afflicted and eventually killed many of the survivors. This is a highly persuasive story in favor of nuclear disarmament. It occupies a unique place in the juvenile literature of the Second World War.

J357 Wakefield, Dan. *Under the Apple Tree, A Novel*. New York: Delacorte/Seymour Lawrence, 1982. 342p.

A patriotic juvenile tale about homefront life in America. The young protagonist is ten-year-old Artie Garber, who lives in a small town in Illinois. His older brother joins the Marines and is sent to the Pacific for combat on Eniwetok and

Guadalcanal. Artie is a patriotic youngster who enthusiastically participates in the paper and scrap-metal drives, victory gardens, defense stamp and bond drives, etc. He also attempts to expose a suspected Japanese spy posing as a Chinese laundryman and a German spy working as an usher in the local movie house. The narrative is filled with nostalgic sights, sounds, songs, slogans, and cliches of the war period in America.

1983

J358   Baer, Frank. *Max's Gang*. Translated by Ivanka Roberts. Boston: Little, Brown, 1983. 298p. [*Die Magermilch-band*. Hamburg: Albrecht Knaus Verlag, 1980.]

During the last days of the war, a group of five German children after being evacuated from their school in Czechoslovakia are sent home. In the confusion of an attack by fighter planes, three of the boys, Adolph, Max, and Peter, become separated from their classmates. But they are determined to find their own way home to Berlin. This is the story of their long and difficult journey and how they fend for themselves by stealing and various other deceptions. The group is caught in a minefield, they are shot at and one is seriously injured by a rock thrown by an irate farmer. The realism of the descriptions is especially grim.

J359   Bograd, Larry. *Los Alamos Light*. New York: Farrar, Straus and Giroux, 1983. 168p.

Sixteen-year-old Maggie Chilton dislikes having to leave Boston and move to New Mexico. The new job of her father will be for the government under the famous physicist Robert Oppenheimer. Maggie knows that his job has something to do with the war. When she arrives in Santa Fe, she discovers that her new home will be in Los Alamos. As she spends time with more friends in the community, she begins to understand why her father must devote so much time to his secret laboratory work. In the process she discovers how much she has come to value her new life. This is a typical didactic juvenile tale designed to encourage responsible behavior and acceptance.

J360   Ferry, Charles. *Raspberry One*. Boston: Houghton Mifflin, 1983. 232p.

This juvenile story concerns the friendships in the Pacific war of two young pilots. Nick and Phil meet two college girls at a servicemen's reception. One of the girls is an artist and she designs the raspberry emblem for the aircraft that the two boys fly. They are soon sent to Iwo Jima, and then to Okinawa, and fly bombing support against the Japanese kamikaze offensive in the Pacific. Despite the letters from home of support and encouragement, the harshness of combat unnerves them, especially Phil. The deaths of men they know and the physical injuries and emotional turmoil experienced substantially changes them. The combat scenes are reliably presented. Much of the plot is based on the wartime experiences of the author when at the age of seventeen, he served as a radioman-gunner on a Navy torpedo bomber. A glossary of flying terms is listed in the back of the book.

J361   Frascino, Edward. *Eddie Spaghetti on the Homefront.* New York: Harper, 1983. 114p.

As the war begins, young Eddie Ferrari, his brother, friends Neil and Gloria, and their neighborhood enemies, the Egan kids, are all caught up in its momentum on the homefront. Eddie collects scrap metal, enjoys air raid drills, and imagines that the local hermit is really a German spy, etc. In essence, this is a reasonably well rendered description of what 1940's Yonkers, New York was like during the war for a ten-year-old boy.

J362   Korschunow, Irina. *A Night in Distant Motion, A Novel.* Translated by Leigh Hafrey. Boston: David Godine, 1983. 158p. [*Er Hiess Jan.* Köln: Benziger Verlag Zürich, 1979.]

This is the first person narrative of seventeen-year-old Regine. She is a German girl who is a good student, loving daughter, and a loyal and obedient supporter of the National Socialist Party. The story begins with an air raid one night in the fall of 1944 when she encounters Jan, a Polish prisoner of war, who pleads with her to help a wounded friend. Her feelings for Jan gradually change from suspicion to curiosity and finally to love. The process leads her to begin to seriously question Nazi doctrine for the first time. She now realizes the full import of the injustice, cruelty, and fear implicit in the life about her. Eventually, someone informs the Gestapo of her illicit relationship with Jan and both are dragged off separately to prison. She escapes from her prison during an air raid and finds refuge at the farm home of a friend at which point she can only wonder about the fate of Jan. This is a perceptive and sensitive view of everyday life in Nazi Germany.

1984

J363   Bilson, Geoffrey. *Hockeybat Harris*. Toronto: Kids Can Press, 1984. 158p.

Some children in England who were evacuated from the cities during the war are sent to Canada for safe keeping. In Canada Bob Williams and his family look forward to hosting an English child. In due course they are sent a boy who turns out to be difficult to handle. The boy David is defensive and quick to express his temper. The narrative describes how Bob Williams comes to see the good side of David underneath his bluster, and is able to create a firm and lasting friendship.

J364   Orlev, Uri. *The Island on Bird Street*. Translated from the Hebrew by Hillel Halkin. Boston: Houghton Mifflin, 1984. c1983. 162p.; London: Hutchinson, 1984. 162p. [*Ha-I Bi-Rehov Ha-Tsiporim*. Jerusalem: Keter, 1981.]

Alex, a Jewish eleven-year-old boy, is from the Warsaw ghetto. His mother was just killed by a Nazi when she was on a visit to Zionist friends. His father works for a rope factory. When the Jews are to be sent away to the camps, Alex is placed in a "selection" which allows another person to sacrifice their life to help others. His father instructs Alex to meet him at a bombed-out shell of a house where the father will come if he can. Every day Alex is forced to forage for food and comb the abandoned houses for supplies. In time he sees his father again at the designated rendezvous spot. The story effectively presents the physical and psychological experiences necessary for ghetto survival.

J365   Tamar, Erika. *Good-bye, Glamour Girl*. New York: Lippincott, 1984. 218p.

Liesl Rosen and her family flee German-occupied Vienna to New York City. The action begins in early 1942. Rita Hayworth becomes her idol as Liesl exhibits all the characteristics and yearnings of a star-struck young girl. A part in a school Christmas play, ethnic friends, and a puppy-love affair with Irish Billy are cast against American popular culture of the war years in New York. The war is ever present as a background element: victory gardens, Russian War Relief,

Morse Code instruction, War Bond drives, and the like. Nonetheless, the primary focus is on the coming of age of Liesl and the abrupt end of her first romantic relationship with a boy.

J366   Todd, Leonard. *The Best Kept Secret of the War*. New York: Knopf, 1984. 165p.

A view of small-town Southern life during the war which concentrates on ten-year-old Cam Reed whose father is off fighting in the war. The father of his playmate is a black marketeer and Cam quickly becomes aware of the various ways some use to further the war effort and others to use it for personal advantage. A nursing-home inmate, his escape with Cam's support, constitute Cam's commitment to what Cam conceives as his personal war effort.

1985

J367   Ferry, Charles. *One More Time!* Boston: Houghton Mifflin, 1985. 171p.

The somewhat vague plot of this episodic juvenile tale features the collective destinies of the members of a popular swing band. Probably the story is influenced by the real-life Glenn Miller band. In any case it is December of 1941 and band leader Gene Markham decides to enlist. The band is on its final tour as more and more of the physically fit members decide to join the various branches of the armed forces. Although the characters seldom are developed into three-dimensional figures, the atmosphere accurately reflects the flavor of the big-band period at its peak and the fears and problems of homefront Americans at the beginning of the war years.

J368   Innocenti, Roberto. *Rose Blanche*. Text by Ian McEwan based on a story by Christophe Gallaz. London: J. Cape, 1985. 30p. [U.S. publication: *Rose Blanche*. Text by Christophe Gallaz and Roberto Innocenti. English translation by Martha Coventry and Richard Graglia. Mankato, MN: Creative Education, 1985. 32p.]

Rose Blanche is a young German girl who watches the beginning of the war and its impact in Germany with youthful obliviousness until one day she hikes into a nearby forest and sees a concentration camp with children among the inmates.

The title also stands for the name of a German wartime protest group. Although this is mainly a picture book it has a matter-of-fact and laconic text that lets the illustrations fill in most of the details of the involvement of Nazi Germany in the war and in its eventual defeat. Since so much of the story is told in pictures a goodly portion of the horror is obscured, e.g., much of what is shown in the pictures--the departing German soldiers, the fat mayor with a swastika on his arm band, starving camp prisoners, etc.--are seen through the uncomprehending eyes of young Rose. It is most likely that adults will need to guide nearly all young readers through these pages for any real understanding and compassion for the nightmare implicit in the provocative book. The artist is Roberto Innocenti while the text by Ian McEwan is taken from a story by Christophe Gallaz.

J369   Ossowski, Leonie. *Star without a Sky*. Translated by Ruth
       Crowley. Minneapolis: Lerner, 1985. 214p. [*Stern Ohne
       Himmel, Roman*. Weinheim: Beltz unt Gelberg, 1978.
       175p.]

The action takes place in a small German village during the final days of the war. A group of German teenagers find Abiram, a young Jewish boy, hiding in a bombed-out building. Willi, a Hitler Youth leader, wants to turn Abiram over to the authorities but some of the others have doubts after Abiram relates his story about the horrors of the concentration camps and the transports. Supposedly based on a true story, the narrative is filled with historical details about just how life was for German civilians as: the Russians gradually approached, refugees flowed through the village, Nazi officials began to flee, and the young people who had wanted to prove their loyalty to the fatherland face defeat and begin to experience grave doubts about their cause. Unfortunately, the story is not very well developed.

J370   Roseman, Kenneth. *Escape from the Holocaust*. New York:
       Union of American Hebrew Congregations, 1985. 179p.

A title in the Do-It-Yourself Jewish Adventure Series that strikes one as bizarre to say the least. The narrative gives the reader options, each with consequences that require further decisions as one fights to survive extermination by the Nazis. At the collapse of the Third Reich, the reader learns what life will be like when one chooses to settle in Israel, America, or a European country. Can there be "an enjoyable way" to "learn about a terrible time in human history?" In spite of the disclaimer, this still seems, indeed, some kind of game. How bizarre.

J371 Vander Els, Betty. *The Bombers' Moon*. New York: Farrar, Straus and Giroux, 1985. 167p.

It is the summer of 1942. Ruth and Simeon, the children of missionaries in central China, are sent by their parents to a school in Loshan away from the invading Japanese. When air attacks begin there the two children are evacuated by air to Calcutta and beyond. It is over four years before they are able to rejoin their parents in Shanghai. The narrative focuses on the day-by-day crises and happenings against the backdrop of the war as the two children are shuttled from one place to another.

1986

J372 Gehrts, Barbara. *Don't Say a Word*. Translated from the German by Elizabeth D. Crawford. New York: Macmillan, 1986. 147p. [*Nie Wieder Ein Wort Davon?* Stuttgart: Union Verlag, 1975. 173p.]

This is an autobiographical tale based on the actual circumstances of the author and her family in Germany during the war years. As young Anna, she describes the life of a German-Jewish family in a Berlin suburb. At first, only the shortages of food and similar stresses of the war are of much concern. But with the restriction on travel, the repressive measures against the Jews and the Allied saturation bombing of Berlin, circumstances worsen dramatically. Although her father is a high-ranking officer in the Luftwaffe he is secretly a participant in the underground activities against the Nazis. In the end he is arrested by the Gestapo and executed. In the meantime, her brother dies in a military hospital of blood poisoning while her sweetheart is killed on the Russian front. This is a rather effective narrative about what it must have been like for ordinary people in the Third Reich during the war years.

J373 Kogawa, Joy. *Naomi's Road*. New York: Oxford University Press, 1986. 82p.

This is the juvenile version by the author of her novel *Obasan* (1981) which describes the evacuation of Japanese Canadians during the war years in Canada. This version is considerably scaled down--less than one-third of the original novel. However, the essential story and characters are retained in a sensitive version for young readers. See the 1981 original adult title for annotation information in *The Novels of World War II: an Annotated Bibliography* (New York: 1993. 2 vols.).

J374   Miner, Jane Claypool. *Veronica*. New York: Scholastic, 1986. 220p.

A juvenile tale placed in Hawaii during and after the Japanese attack on Pearl Harbor. Not seen.

J375   Tripp, Valerie. *Meet Molly, An American Girl*. Madison, WI: Pleasant Company, 1986. 58p.

The third series of the author in The American Girls Collection focuses on a young girl called Molly who dreams and schemes on the homefront during the war. There are five titles [items J375, J376, J377, J381, and J390] in the series. They are basic, didactic, and simple stories for young girls based on everyday events and problems with ample illustrations and drawings scattered throughout the texts. This first one shows Molly's reactions to eating victory-garden vegetables and her Halloween disappointments caused by her little brother as her conflicts during the war.

J376   Tripp, Valerie. *Molly Learns a Lesson, A School Story*. Madison, WI: Pleasant Company, 1986. 67p.

The second Molly story of The American Girls Collection describes nine-year-old Molly as she and her friends at school try to aid the United States war effort. See item J375 for details on this juvenile series.

J377   Tripp, Valerie. *Molly's Surprise, A Christmas Story*. Madison, WI: Pleasant Company, 1986. 64p.

The third Molly title in The American Girls Collection describes how her father serving in a hospital in England finds a way to make the Christmas celebration of Molly and the family a very special occasion even though he is so far away. See item J375 for a description of the series.

J378   Watkins, Yoko Kawashima. *So Far From the Bamboo Grove*. New York: Lothrop, Lee & Shepard, 1986. 183p.

It is early 1945 and the Pacific war has now come to north eastern Korea. Eight-year-old Yoko, a Japanese girl, and her mother and older sister flee from the advancing Communists to Seoul where they hope to reach her grandparents in Japan. For the next few months they are refugees subject to all the uncertainties and potential violence of the times. Desperate to escape, they finally succeed and reach Japan only to discover that the grandparents have been killed in the U.S. bombings. This is an autobiographical story that eloquently describes the resolute determination and ingenuity of the sisters, even after their mother dies in the quest to return home to Japan. This is an unusual setting and theme seldom if ever employed in any other juvenile novel or story. There is no comparable adult novel.

1987

J379 Matas, Carol. *Lisa*. Toronto: Lester and Orpen Dennys, 1987. 123p. [Title in U.S.: *Lisa's War*. New York: Scribner, 1989. 111p.]

The action begins in Copenhagen in 1940. Lisa, a twelve-year-old Jewish girl, is the protagonist. She and her brother join the Danish resistance after the Germans invade Denmark. Stefan, the brother, becomes involved in sabotage missions against the German-run factories while Lisa and her girl friend help to distribute resistance pamphlets. After her girl friend's parents are killed by the Germans, Lisa devotes herself wholeheartedly to resistance activities. The action covers a three-year period and describes how thousands of Jews fled Denmark to avoid death and deportation. Lisa and her brother help in this escape process to Sweden. The fictional narrative is related in the first person by Lisa and is reminiscent of the diary of Anne Frank. This is an effective Jewish resistance story for juveniles.

J380 Noonan, Michael. *McKenzie's Boots*. St. Lucia, Queensland: University of Queensland Press, 1987. 239p.; New York: Orchard Books, 1988. 249p.

Here is a young adult story featuring fifteen-year-old Rod, a tall, muscular Australian boy who talks his way into the Australian Army by pretending to be older than he is. The first part of the story charts his efforts to be accepted into the army and quickly establishes his innocence along with his special physical characteristics such as his size 13 shoes. Part Two covers his platoon's combat assignment to fight the Japanese in the jungles of New Guinea. In the end when Rod is killed the Japanese take his enormous boots as a souvenir from a soldier they consider a hero. There are many incidents of combat but there is a distinct tendency to glorify and romanticize the process of battle in terms of individual acts of heroism rather than the daily grind and horror of jungle combat.

J381   Tripp, Valerie. *Happy Birthday, Molly! A Springtime Story.* Madison, WI: Pleasant Company, 1987. 64p.

The fourth Molly story in The American Girl Collection depicts how an English girl comes to stay with the family in America and how Molly comes to understand and appreciate cultural differences. See item J375 for a more complete description of this series.

1988

J382   Baklanov, Grigorii Iakovievich. *Forever Nineteen.* Translated by Antonia W. Bouis. New York: Lippincott, 1989. 168p. [*Naveki-deviatnadtsatiletnie.* Okliabr, 1979.]

The story relates with sensitivity the reactions and fate of a nineteen-year-old Russian lieutenant on the Eastern front. Lt. Tretyakov doesn't last even through his first battle before he is wounded. Most of the action occurs in the hospital ward where he recovers amidst the blinded and maimed Russian troopers. He falls in love with a girl from the nearby village while a constant flow of crowded troop trains passes by on their way to the front. When he returns to his unit, and then combat again, he is almost accidentally killed. The battle scenes are stark and brutally realistic. The story is based on the experiences of the author who perceptively describes not only the battle episodes but also the complex emotions of his protagonist both in battle and in the hospital behind the lines. Although this is classed as a juvenile story, it should hold ample interest for anyone interested in the war.

J383   Bawden, Nina. *Henry.* New York: Lothrop, Lee and Shepard, 1988. 119p.

A sensitive tale about the evacuation of a twelve-year-old girl, her mother and two brothers from London to the Jones family farm in the English countryside. They find a baby orphan squirrel to whom they give the name Henry. In brief, the narrative describes how Henry is raised and loved, and how he is one day accidentally released back into the countryside from his cage. On another level the squirrel comes to symbolize all that the family has lost in its evacuation--stability, carefreeness, youth--but with the hope of change and freedom.

J384   Childress, Mark. *V for Victor*. New York: Knopf, 1989, c1988. 320p.

The time is 1942. Sixteen-year-old Victor has been sent by his family to stay with his aged grandmother on an island in Mobile Bay, Alabama. The war has its effect everywhere: school, home, the community. One night Victor hears a peculiar sound out on the Bay and decides to investigate on his own. He discovers a German sub and soon finds himself in the middle of a Nazi plot. He is alternately a hostage and then in pursuit of the enemy. This is a coming-of-age juvenile tale with a contrived and often farfetched plot.

J385   Heuck, Sigrid. *The Hideout*. Translated from the German by Rika Lesser. New York: Dutton, 1988. 183p. [*Maisfrieden*. Stuttgart: K. Thienemanns, 1986.]

This is a bizarre but exceptional juvenile fantasy. It is the last year of the war in a German city. A young girl is found in the rubble. She can only remember her first name, Rebecca. The German officials send her to live at an orphanage. But when her train is stopped for an air raid, she flees into a nearby cornfield. There she meets a mysterious boy called Sami who lives alone in a bomb crater. She is paralyzed with fear during the many bombing raids but he seems fearless and rescues her from her anxieties by taking her to a land of fantasy where it is warm with plenty of food and there is no war. Even when she is found and taken to live at the orphanage, she continues to visit Sami and partakes in his fantasy trips where rich meals and the mouse-kings are more real than the battles and bombs of wartime. The writing is sensitive and extremely effective in revealing the war through the eyes of a child.

J386   Marshall, Heather. *Anneliese*. London: Hodder and Stoughton, 1988. 252p.

This is basically a juvenile story about the coming of age of an overweight, emotionally deprived adolescent girl. Shona retreats into her dream world where she creates an alter ego she calls Anneliese who is everything she wants to be. Shona becomes a diet fanatic, revolts against her mother in typical adolescent fashion which results in a tragic conclusion. The narrative has a background of New Zealand at war: rationing, fear of the Japanese invasion, and the influx of the American troops and their impact on New Zealand women and society.

J387 Roth-Hano, Renee. *Touch Wood: A Girlhood in Occupied France*. New York: Four Winds Press, 1988. 297p.

The time is 1940 and Renee Roth, a nine-year-old French schoolgirl of Jewish heritage, narrates the story of her family and their forced exile from Alsace to Paris. The parents assure Renee and her two sisters that now things will not get any worse ("touch wood") but they obviously do. Curfews, the yellow star, the prospect of the camps and deportation cause the parents to send their three daughters away to Normandy to live secretly with nuns. At first a safe haven, there is a developing confusion by the girls over their religious identity. The terrible bombings when the Allies finally invade in 1944 cause fear and devastation over the French countryside. The narrative is couched in the form of a juvenile diary which records the impressions of Renee on the treatment of the Jews, the Nazi occupation, and a host of related conditions in occupied France. This is an autobiographical novel based on the personal experiences of the author.

J388 Southall, Ivan. *Blackbird*. New York: Farrar Straus Giroux, 1988. 135p.

Here is a fiction that demonstrates the impact of the war on an Australian family on the homefront. The time is 1942. Will, his older brother and mother move inland from the northern coast to avoid any possible Japanese invasion attack. Will is the central character who becomes involved in his own private war games. The plot is immaterial whereas the characterization is all. An unnamed narrator tells the tale which begins after the father has moved the family inland. One day when Will is climbing on the roof of the house, he falls and injures his leg. This incident causes a fear of climbing. The death of a young blackbird followed by the bizarre response of another blackbird serve to let Will know that some risks may not be worth taking. This is a complex story that may well elude the understanding of most young readers.

J389 Temperley, Alan. *Murdo's War*. Edinburgh: Canongate, 1988. 264p.

It is 1943 on the isolated northern coast of Scotland. The people are fully expecting to be invaded by the Germans. Young Murdo has lost his mother and his father is in military service. Murdo lives and works for an old and crusty fisherman who also runs whiskey at night. When an English city slicker hires the old fisherman to smuggle crates, Murdo soon uncovers a Nazi plot. The boy is then forced to flee south to escape his German pursuers and reach English authorities. In effect, this is a thriller adventure tale with all the trappings of this genre. The narrative is carefully constructed with realistic characters and events coupled with artful descriptions.

J390 Tripp, Valerie. *Changes for Molly, A Winter Story*. Madison, WI: Pleasant Company, 1988. 67p.

The fifth (and last) story in The American Girls Collection series describes how Molly copes with life and school during the final months after her father announces his transfer home from the war and military duty in England. In effect, this is a view of American homefront life from the perspective of a young twelve-year-old girl. The advance notice of her father's return home makes it especially difficult for Molly to perform in the patriotic show put on by the school. The illustrations, particularly in the didactic epilogue (with its instructional, nonfiction text) summarizes the impact of the war on American civilian life. See item J375 for additional information about the Molly series.

J391 Yolen, Jane. *The Devil's Arithmetic*. New York: Viking Kestrel, 1988. 170p.

This is an innovative switch on the typical world of fantasy time-travel fiction. In this case, Hannah, the twelve-year-old heroine, is transported back to Poland during the Nazi holocaust period after she finds the annual family Seder in New York state tedious and dull. When selected to perform the Jewish ritual of opening the door to Elijah, she finds herself in 1942 rural Poland and with the name of Chaya. There she shares the experiences of Jewish villagers who are soon transported by train to a concentration camp. She learns that some must bear witness to these horrors. When her new friend Rivka is about to be sent to the ovens, Hannah as Chaya goes in her place - only to awake and find herself back home at the family Seder. This is a sensitive and creative narrative which compassionately and forthrightly explores the consequences and meaning of the holocaust. A well written and superior tale that every child should read (and their parents as well).

1989

J392   Green, Connie Jordan. *The War at Home*. New York: Margaret K. McElderry Books, 1989. 136p.

This juvenile novel is placed in Oak Ridge, Tennessee in 1944 and 1945. Mattie McDowell is the thirteen-year-old heroine who is more affected by the war against her visiting cousin than the one against the Japanese or the Germans. Her father has just taken a top-secret job in the newly created town whose borders are guarded by soldiers day and night. Although the story portrays the mystery of the new town and the cramped and crowded small houses, the plot focuses mostly on Mattie and her cousin Virgil, who comes to spend several months with her family and generates the personality war between the two children. The story does not explore the use of atomic energy for weapons or the ethical dilemma associated with its development.

J393   Laird, Christa. *Shadow of the Wall*. London: MacRae Books, 1989. 134p.

This holocaust tale is directed to juveniles. All alone in the world, Misha and his sister Rachel have lived in an orphanage in the Warsaw ghetto. Conditions have grown steadily worse so that Misha is forced to become a smuggler on the black market. However, he is recruited by an underground resistance group just in time to escape being sent to Treblinka. It is clear the narrative is based on the actual experiences of the author in the Warsaw ghetto. Unfortunately, the story is awkwardly constructed with many apparently arbitrary point-of-view changes. Even Misha's story seems an add-on so as to appeal more to juvenile readers. Nonetheless, the sad, ugly truth is obvious about the claustrophobia of the doomed lives in the ghetto.

J394   Lingard, Joan. *Tug of War*. London: Hamish Hamilton, 1989. 186p.; New York: Lodestar, 1990. 194p.

The scene commences in Latvia in 1944. The Peterson family decides to flee to safety and leaves for Leipzig where they hope to stay with an old friend. While traveling through Poland, fourteen-year-old Hugo is separated from the rest of the family who are forced to continue their journey when they cannot find him. Contrast and suspense are developed by alternating from Hugo's adventures (and resuce by the Schneider family) to those of his twin sister, Astra. Over half of the narrative covers the war years with the final seventy pages on the immediate postwar period. Hugo is finally reunited with his family in Hamburg only to discover that the Schneiders have by now assumed a similar relationship to him when he must decide whether to accompany his sister and family to Canada, or remain with the Schneiders in Germany. A reasonably accurate view of day to day life in war-torn Europe from 1944 to 1947.

J395   Lowry, Lois. *Number the Stars*. Boston: Houghton Mifflin, 1989. 137p.; London: Dent, 1989. 128p.

When Denmark is occupied by the Germans, ten-year-old Annemarie and Ellen, her best friend, are confronted by two patrolling enemy soldiers which brings the war close to home. This and the news that the Jews are being rounded up frightens them and their families. Ellen's family flees immediately leaving her in the care of a sympathetic Danish family who shield her when the Nazis raid their apartment. The narrative continues along this line emphasizing the many efforts to smuggle Jews into Sweden. Well written with considerable suspense.

J396   Matas, Carol. *Jesper*. Toronto: Lester and Orpen Dennys, 1989. 152p. [Title in U.S.: *Code Name Kris*. New York: Scribner, 1990. 152p.]

Continues the story about resistance activities in Denmark as begun in *Lisa* (or *Lisa's War*) item J338. After helping many Danish Jews to escape the Nazi roundup by reaching neutral Sweden, seventeen-year-old Jesper goes underground to avoid German reprisals against his family. He uses the code name "Kris" as he employs resistance newspapers and sabotage attempts to undermine the German occupying force. This leads to emotional crises and opposition even within the Danish resistance, especially when his Jewish friend Stefan returns from Sweden on a special mission and competitive emotions surface within Jesper as he comes to acknowledge his love for both girls, Lisa and Janicke, when Janicke is murdered by the Germans. There is plenty of drama and covert action to entrance the juvenile reader.

J397   Pearson, Kit. *The Sky is Falling*. Markham, Ontario; New York: Viking Kestrel, 1989. 248p.

When the Germans begin to bomb England ten-year-old Norah and her five-year-old brother are sent by their parents over their objections to Toronto, Canada for safekeeping. Norah's personality-clash with their sponsor, a wealthy widow, results in her deepening resentment and resistance. The point of this well written narrative is to show how children were traumatized by the evacuations caused by the war.

J398   Prins, Piet. *The Partisans*. Neerlandia, Alta.: Inheritance Publishers, 1989. 102p.

About the Dutch resistance activities during the German occupation. Not seen.

J399   Prins, Piet. *Sabotage*. Neerlandia, Alta.: Inheritance Press, 1989. 120p.

More about the Dutch resistance activities during the German occupation. Not seen.

J400   Sevela, Ephraim. *We Were Not Like Other People*. Translated from the Russian by Antonina W. Bouis. New York: Harper and Row, 1989. 216p.

A nameless Soviet boy who is Jewish recounts the events of his life from the age of nine when his officer father is swallowed by Stalin's purges of 1937. He describes his years (to 1946) of nightmarish wanderings with first his mother and sister, and then alone primarily in Eastern Europe and Russia. He is interned at a vocational school where starving orphans collapse into death-dealing machines, and experiences a freezing journey through the steppes in an empty coal car. His stint as a farm laborer in Siberia brings only a sort of material relief. He is sent next to the German front as a colonel's would-be adoptive son only to be orphaned again by the time the war is over. The translation is superb with a powerful prose style that is sensitive and genuine.

J401   Westall, Robert. *Blitzcat*. New York: Scholastic, 1989. 230p.

Probably this is best classified as a juvenile tale which describes the British homefront as seen through the eyes of a black cat called Lord Gort. The cat searches war ravaged England for her beloved master who is an RAF pilot. The cat travels from Dover under threat of invasion to Coventry, flies as mascot with British bombers over France, survives a parachute drop, and eventually returns to England and finds her master. Seemingly fanciful, the tale is nevertheless well done with an animal survival appeal similar to that of *The Incredible Journey*.

1990

J402 Chang, Margaret and Raymond. *In the Eye of War*. New York: Margaret K. McElderry Books, 1990. 198p.

This is autobiographical fiction based on the lives of the authors during the Japanese occupation of Shanghai. The primary character, ten-year-old Shao-shao, seems little affected by the war. Although his older brother has been taken away for forced labor, he is scarcely concerned since he never especially liked him. The main interests of the little boy are cricket fights, his silk worms, and the little girl across the courtyard. Although the little boy watches the American air raids on the docks and Japanese shipping, the main tragedy in his life is the loss of his pet bird. Thus, there is a strange sense of unreality about this so-called wartime juvenile tale. But perhaps just that, indeed, is the nature of childhood.

J403 Glassman, Judy. *The Morning Glory War*. New York: Dutton's Childrens Books, 1990. 119p.

Relates how eleven-year-old Jeannie copes with the impact of the war on her Brooklyn homefront. In a school letter writing project to servicemen, she is the only one to find a pen pal who turns out to be a dream boat. The narrative recreates the shabby wartime neighborhood, the air-raid drills, the shortages of foods, characteristic social activities, and various petty school jealousies of her harsh teacher and fellow students, and even the vandalization of her window box of morning glories.

J404 Morpurgo, Michael. *Waiting for Anya*. London: Heinemann, 1990. 172p.

Here is a story of adventure placed in Vichy France. The protagonist is Jo, a young shepherd boy, who becomes involved in smuggling Jewish children over the border into Spain. Benjamin, the son-in-law of the widow Horcada, has been hiding Jewish children at her farm near Jo's village. Benjamin has also been waiting for his daughter, Anya, to arrive through the help of the underground. They have been separated for nearly two years after escaping a German attack in Paris. When the Germans suddenly occupy Jo's village, the smuggling operation becomes even more risky. Nonetheless, all of the villagers become involved in helping the last group of children to escape, but Benjamin and one child are caught and sent to die at Auschwitz. At the end of the war Anya finally arrives safely at the farm in a conclusion that combines success and tragedy reflective of the fate of actual wartime victims.

J405 Pfeffer, Wendy. *The Gooney War*. White Hall, VA: Shoe Tree Press, 1990. 48p.

Describes the struggle of the U.S. Navy to keep its air base on Midway Island clear of the disruptive albatrosses, or gooney birds, immediately before and during the war. The birds continually interfere with the landing and take-off of aircraft. The dilemma is finally resolved when an officer comes up with a clever solution which results at last in a peaceful coexistence.

J406 Poynter, Margaret. *A Time Too Swift*. New York: Atheneum, 1990. 216p.

A narrative about fifteen-year-old Marjorie whose innocent dreams about war and men in uniform become affected by the people about her that she loves and cares for, e.g. a friend's father dies at Pearl Harbor; another is classified 4F and accused of cowardice; a Japanese classmate and her family are interned; her brother is wounded overseas, etc.

J407 Ray, Deborah Kogan. *My Daddy Was a Soldier, A World War II Story*. New York: Holiday House, 1990. 40p.

Jeannie's father joins the army when she is in the third grade. Her mother becomes a welder at the local navy yard and her life becomes occupied with ration books and their red and blue stamps, food shortages, victory gardens, scrap-metal drives, and blackouts. The text has ample pencil drawings especially calculated to appeal to young children.

J408 Townsend, Tom. *The Hooligans*. Austin, TX: Eakin Press, 1990. 116p.

A group of orphans run away from their institution to take part in the war effort. They become the crew for a schooner patrolling the Atlantic coast looking for German subs. Not seen.

J409 Treseder, Terry Walton. *Hear O Israel, A Story of the Warsaw Ghetto*. New York: Atheneum, 1990. 41p.

The action starts in the Warsaw Ghetto. It is the narrative of Isaac, a young Jewish boy who is steadfast in his belief in God. Isaac describes the illusions held by his father who believes the Jews must wait for God; the disaffection and loss of faith by his older brother; and the final terrible moments before his own death at Treblinka. This is a brief and disturbing narrative that well captures the troubling and dismaying events of this horrible time. It should be a valuable dose of reality for many young readers.

J410   Van Kirk, Eileen. *A Promise to Keep*. New York: Lodestar, 1990. 147p.

Fourteen-year-old Ellie and her older sister are sent in 1940 from London to the farm of cousins to spend the summer away from the Battle of Britain. Both girls but especially Ellie are entranced by the advances of Curt, a handsome young Austrian refugee working nearby. When Curt rescues and hides a wounded German pilot who has parachuted nearby, Ellie responds positively to his need for help. The delimma of Ellie is made reasonably understandable when she decides to remain loyal to Curt (in spite of his pro-German sympathies) rather than turn him and the wounded pilot over to the military authorities. Although the author makes a case for Ellie's behavior, the blanket blindness of the patriotic English to Curt's loyalty to the German Reich is a bit far fetched to countenance even in a juvenile novel such as this. Insufficient attention is given to the nature of promises, ethics, and hard choices especially in war time. Young love is no excuse for such contructs of flabby character as presented by this author; presumably as a sympathetic model of behavior for juveniles.

J411   Westall, Robert. *The Kingdom by the Sea*. London: Methuen Children's, 1990. 175p.

The war background is the catalyst for the process of self discovery and survival of twelve-year-old Harry, the protagonist. When his home in north England is destroyed in a 1942 bombing raid and Harry believes all of his family have been killed, he sets out to find his way in the world rather than be sent to live with relatives he thoroughly dislikes. He soon is joined by a homeless dog. Together they travel but Harry quickly learns that there are all too many less than well-intentioned people in the world such as the perverted Corporal Merman who are ready to exploit him. Finally, he finds refuge with a caring school teacher whose son has been killed in the war. Here at his home, Harry finds what he calls his "kingdom by the sea." Nonetheless, he soon learns his family are all alive. Harry's maturing travels forever create a nostalgic memory for his newfound spiritual home by the sea. The story concludes with the prospect that Harry will one day be liberated from his ignorant and insensitive parents and return. His travels, experiences, and self-quest for survival, both physical and spiritual, are expertly drawn by the author in endearing prose, and placed all the more in sharp contrast by the effects of the war.

J412   Westall, Robert. *The Promise*. London: Macmillan, 1990.
       169p.; New York: Scholastic, 1991. 169p.

This supernatural tale about life after death is set in England during the Blitz. A young teenager, Bob Bickerstaffe, encounters his first girl friend in the frail but pretty Valerie. Although this all occurs during the Battle of Britain which consumes most of Bob's interest, he is nevertheless stunned when Valerie dies. When he visits her now vacant house, he comes under the spell of her ghost which reminds him of his promise and nearly drives him to his grave. Images of death are a dominant feature of the story ranging from his visit to a cemetery with his grandmother through the frightening air battles overhead, to the attempts of Valerie's ghost to take him with her into the other world. The background is life in England during the war but the supernatural plot of young love strains one's credulity in this bizarre mixture of fantasy and realism, in spite of the careful and capable writing.

J413   Woolf, Betty. *Call Me Aunt*. Nashville, TN: Winston-Derek,
       1990. 132p.

Describes the experiences of twelve-year-old Sophie when she is evacuated from her home in London to live in the countryside with a kindly elderly woman, Not seen.

1991

J414   Aaron, Chester. *Alex, Who Won His War*. New York: Walker,
       1991. 156p.

This is a thriller-type story placed in a coastal town in Connecticut during 1945 before the end of the war in Europe. Fourteen-year-old Alex is forced into silence by two German spies who have taken over the nearby house of two elderly neighbors and holds them hostage. While Alex misses his brother who is involved in the Battle of the Bulge, he is torn between his loyalty to his brother and his growing regard for one of the Germans. The wartime background is rendered with care and authenticity. The story is well constructed with credible suspense.

J415   Bergman, Tamar. *Along the Tracks.* Translated from the Hebrew by Michael Swirsky. Boston: Houghton Mifflin, 1991. 245p. [*Le-orekh ha-mesilah.* Jerusalem: Shoken, 1987. 223p.]

These fictional adventures about Yankele, a small eight-year-old Jewish boy constantly on the move in Russia during the war years, are based on the actual experiences of a friend of the author. The story begins with a third-person account of the escape from Lodz, and the trek across Poland to the Russian border. The saga continues at this point by the first-person account of Yankele. He has been separated from his family, and now begins an exhausting journey of four years through the countryside, hiking and riding freight trains while attempting to find his mother. In the process he encounters other abandoned children. This is a startling and intense view of the impact of the war on a young boy who is determined to survive at all costs, and does.

J416   Choi, Sook Nyul. *Year of Impossible Goodbyes.* Boston: Houghton Mifflin, 1991. 171p.

The first half of this short tale takes place during the six months or so before the Japanese surrender in 1945. Ten-year-old Sookan, her mother, and her younger brother have survived the cruelties and misery of the Japanese occupation of Korea. Her father has been a resistance fighter who is now hiding in Manchuria while her older brothers have been sent to Japanese labor camps. When the war ends the Russians and the Korean Communists take over North Korea. Sookan and her family decide their only chance to survive is to escape to the south, but only Sookan and her little brother are able to cross the 38th parallel and eventually reach freedom. The bitter cruelties of everyday life under the Japanese occupation are realistically presented including the school sessions conducted by Japanese teachers for Korean children, and the removal of the Korean "sock girls" from their knitting factory to be sent to the front to serve as sex slaves for the Japanese troops. The narrative is simply stated but with a realistic power that seizes the attention and sympathy of the reader.

J417 Hahn, Mary Downing. *Stepping on the Cracks.* New York: Clarion Books, 1991. 216p.

It is August of 1944 and Margaret, the eleven-year-old narrator along with her friend Elizabeth, are prone to shouting: "Step on a crack, break Hitler's back." Both girls have brothers in the war and are extremely patriotic. They also despise the local bully. When the girls learn he is hiding his older brother who is a deserter, they decide to get revenge by threatening exposure. The narrative now explores the issue of pacifism sympathetically and both girls become interested and supportive of the plight of the bully's brother. This realization is matched with the bitter contempt of the parents for all deserters, the death of Margaret's brother in the war, and the complexity of life even for an eleven-year-old under such circumstances. This is a fearless and blunt look at choices with no easy out ending or facile conclusion.

J418 Herman, Charlotte. *A Summer on Thirteenth Street.* New York: Dutton Children's Books, 1991. 181p.

Shirley Cohen, the eleven-year-old protagonist, is living in Chicago. It is 1944 and Shirley is looking forward to a summer of play with her friends. But pets can die and her German spy suspect will turn out to be a harmless and kindly man. The narrative artfully captures the homefront atmosphere in Chicago while revealing in the protagonist the tensions between childhood and emerging adolescence. The author provides a background with plenty of realistic period detail.

J419 Hest, Amy. *Love You, Soldier.* New York: Four Winds Press, 1991. 47p.

This first-person narrative is placed in New York City during the war years. Seven-year-old Katie misses her soldier father who has just been shipped off to battle. This story is an account of Katie's resourcefulness under the pressures of wartime and the resulting effects on her family life. The early 1940s are evoked as witnessed through the eyes and concerns of a young child. The death of her father dramatically changes the nature of her family life as well as her reaction to the eventual remarriage of her mother. This is a simple but believable tale about love and the nature of family life during the war years in America.

J420   Hoobler, Thomas and Dorothy. *Aloha Means Come Back: The Story of a World War II Girl.* Englewood Cliffs, N.J.: Silver Burdett, 1991. 55p.

Placed at Pearl Harbor, the protagonist Laura, the daughter of an American Naval officer, finds that the Japanese-American neighbors are loyal, helpful, and brave as any other group of citizens. Laura and her mother join her officer father in Hawaii in 1941 at a time when many Hawaiians expect that there will be war with Japan and, as a consequence, are suspicious of any citizen of Japanese heritage. When Pearl Harbor is bombed, Laura's mother is injured. The journey to the hospital with the assistance of Laura's Japanese friend Michiko re-emphasizes the basic goodness of Japanese-Americans. The narrative concludes with a short chapter on how to make a lei. This is a simple and didactic tale with a generally convincing historical background that endeavors to show how the lives of ordinary people were effected by the war.

J421   Kudlinski, Kathleen V. *Pearl Harbor is Burning! A Story of World War II.* New York: Viking Penguin, 1991. 54p.

A young boy, Frank Hopkins, has just recently moved to Hawaii. He has no friends and is taunted by the local boys as an outsider. Kenji, a Japanese-American boy, offers his friendship when they discover a lot in common such as baseball. The two are in Frank's tree house overlooking Pearl Harbor when the Japanese attack. They watch the battle from this dramatic vantage point. When Frank's mother who is a nurse must report to the hospital, Kenji's family takes in Frank as a friendly gesture. The prejudice of Frank's mother is used as a didactic theme when Frank discovers that a Japanese-American boy can be a "real friend." The story illustrates not only an actual historical event but also the multicultural tolerance of Hawaiian society as compared with the West coast of mainland America. The tale commemorates the fiftieth anniversary of the attack on Pearl Harbor. This is a workmanlike narrative which at times can seem contrived.

J422   Magorian, Michelle. *Not a Swan.* London: Methuen, 1991. 384p.

This is a coming-of-age story for adolescent girls. This dominant theme is only incidentally related to the war. Seventeen-year-old Roe (short for Rose) and her two older sisters are evacuated to a small English seaside house to stay for several months while their actress mother is off on an overseas assignment with the E.N.S.A. Nearly all of the sentimental plot concerns Roe's adolescent fantasy life based on a diary she has found in the cottage. She has her first love affair, helps an unwed pregnant girl, and begins to discover her talents as a writer. The war serves mainly as the cause for Roe's relocation to the seaside cottage. Otherwise the story could have been placed at nearly any other time and place during the last sixty-five years.

J423   Marvin, Isabel R. *Bridge to Freedom.* Philadelphia: Jewish Publication Society, 1991. 136p.

The time is March 1945, close to the end of the war in Europe. Kurt, a fifteen-year-old German Army deserter, reluctantly joins up with Rachel, a Jewish girl refugee, and her wounded dog in order to cross into Belgium to safety. The bridge of the title refers to the bridge at Remagen which the Germans have failed to destroy. This is the bridge which Kurt and Rachel must cross for any hope of freedom. Their planning and efforts to cross the bridge, their success, and separation on the other side of the river until they accidentially meet again in Liege, form the suspense and drama of this war adventure with a message.

J424   Mellecker, Judith. *Randolph's Dream.* New York: Knopf, 1991. 40p.

The young boy Randolph has been sent from London to stay with relatives in the countryside during the Blitz. He helps in the garden, saves string, and pursues his hobbies of stamp and moth collecting. In his sleep he dreams at first that he flies around the nearby country side. Then he flies to North Africa where his father is stationed and later lost in the desert. Randolph then saves his father and takes home an orange which he finds in his pocket in the morning when he awakes. This is a fantasy story about a child who finds a magical refuge from his emotional distress.

J425   Orlev, Uri. *The Man from the Other Side.* Translated from the Hebrew by Hillel Halkin. Boston: Houghton Mifflin, 1991. 186. [*Ish Min Ha-tsad Ha-aher.* Jerusalem: Keter, 1988. 143p.]

Marek, the fourteen-year-old narrator, describes and even participates in the anti-Semitism promoted by the Nazis in occupied Warsaw. Then he discovers that his father was

Jewish. This so shocks him that he resolves to aid the Jews in the ghetto. When the Warsaw ghetto uprising begins, Marek is caught in the fighting as he guides his stepfather through the sewers to and from the ghetto. This truly seems to be an appropriate metaphor for the underworld of the human self and the dangers faced from within and from without. That this is a most penetrating and carefully constructed work of fiction is obvious. The translation is superb.

J426 Paulsen, Gary. *The Cookcamp.* New York: Orchard Books, 1991. 115p.

The action is placed in the forests of Minnesota in 1944. A road is under construction towards the Canadian border. A young boy arrives from Chicago at the local railroad station to live with his grandmother who cooks for the construction crew. He misses his mother and his father who is off in the war, but nonetheless helps out on the road construction project. The war is a distant factor in this story about isolation, homesickness, and the memory of an extraordinary immigrant grandmother who came from Norway as a young girl. The action is related in a sensitive and nostalgic prose.

J427 Vos, Ida. *Hide and Seek.* Translated by Terese Edelstein and Inez Smidt. Boston: Houghton Mifflin, 1991.132p. [*Wie Niet Weg Is Wordt Gezien.* Den Haag: Leopold, 1981. 151p.]

This is an autobiographical novel about the experiences of a Jewish family during the German occupation of Holland. The time is 1940 and eight-year-old Rachel Hartog becomes aware of the changes in her world: blackout drills, curfews, anti-semitic policies and symbols (the yellow stars), and restricted access for Jews. Rachel and her family decide to go into hiding after a number of Jewish children are taken away by the Germans. The narrative makes clear that many Netherlanders took risks to shelter Jews and specifically Rachel's family. Everyone lives under a heavy burden of fear of discovery. When the war is finally over, Rachel's family at last are able to be together again, but Rachel is soon preoccupied in counting the number of family members lost in the camps and in the war. The grief and suffering of the people is forthrightly presented.

J428 Wild, Margaret. *Let the Celebrations Begin!* London: Bodley Head, 1991. 32p.; New York: Orchard Books, 1991. 1 vol. [Title page verso information indicates this was first published by Omnibus Books in Norwood, Australia.]

This is a picture-book with a first-person narrative by a young woman prisoner of the Bergen Belsen concentration camp. The brief text tells how a handful of camp women used scraps of cloth torn from their own skimpy clothing to make stuffed toys as gifts to be given to the few children left alive when the camp is liberated. Unfortunately, any reader without additional background on this sorry and miserable Nazi period will be unable fully to comprehend the true meaning of the story in spite of the few quotations scattered throughout the book. Only readers acquainted with the history of the Nazi holocaust will be able to understand this somewhat hermetic tribute to the courageous women of the camp who never abandoned hope. It is difficult to see how young children on their own could ever begin to grasp the import of this narrative, especially with the illustrations which seem to strongly romanticize their subjects.

J429   Wild, Margaret. *A Time for Toys*. Toronto: Kids Can Press, 1991. 32p.

Describes life in the concentration camps during the war. Not seen. Unavailable for interlibrary loan.

J430   Yolen, Jane. *All Those Secrets of the World*. Boston: Little, Brown, 1991. 32p.

A children's picture-book based on an autobiographical episode from the childhood of the author. Four-year-old Janie and her cousin see her father off to war on a troopship. She gets a plentitude of kisses, waves the flag, and is treated to ice cream. The next day when she and her cousin are at her grandparent's beach, Janie is frightened when her cousin runs off to demonstrate to her how everything appears smaller when far away - one of the "secrets of the world" he says. Two years later when her father returns and comments on how much bigger she is, Janie shares her secret, namely, she is bigger now than then because he is here and not far away. The illustrations are in a watercolor style that perfectly conveys the nostalgic flavor of the war period on the East coast, while the brief text is almost poetic in its impact.

1992

J431   Ackerman, Karen. *When Mama Retires*. New York: Knopf, 1992. 36p.

The title refers to the probability that the mother will retire from housework and take a job in a wartime factory. Mainly a picture-book, the text covers a day in the life of a family whose father is away in the army. The oldest son describes how his mother instructs her three boys in how to do the daily housework just in case she should become a riveter in the local aircraft company. The text is brief but convincing in its description of the consternation of the children when they learn life can change so unexpectedly as a consequence of the war. The drawings are effective in reinforcing the instability of life theme of the text.

J432   Dillon, Eilis. *Children of Bach*. New York: Scribner, 1992. 164p.

The plot is set in wartime Budapest during the German occupation. Fourteen-year-old Peter returns home from school with his younger sister and brother only to discover that his famous musician parents have been taken prisoner by the Nazis in a local Jewish roundup. The children try to obtain consolation by making music together when their aunt mysteriously returns home after tricking her would-be captors. Although the parents never return, the children are sustained by the hope that they will return once the war is over. There is some suspense but the Nazis and their Hungarian supporters seem too easily duped. The fear and anxiety which was the lot of any Jewish family seems too far removed from this narrative to reflect accurately the grim realities that even a young reader should frankly confront still today over fifty years after the end of the war.

J433   Holmes, Mary Z. *Dear Dad*. Austin, Texas: Raintree/Steck-Vaughn, 1992. 48p.

The first-person narrative is placed in Miami Beach, Florida mostly during 1942. The protagonist is Max, a junior high school student, who does his utmost to help the war effort particularly when his dad goes to fight overseas. Max is from a Jewish family which provides the author with an opportunity to stress the fate of European Jews under the Nazis. Chapters are named for some of the months of the year and each begins with a brief letter from Max to his father. The text reveals the everyday news of the war and the concerns of an average American family. The number of illustrations are such that this work tends to fall into the picture-book genre.

J434   Marko, Katherine. *Hang Out the Flag.* New York: Macmillan, 1992. 159p.

It is September of 1943 and little eleven-year-old Leslie is eagerly awaiting the return on leave of her father who is in the Navy Seabees and soon due to be shipped overseas. The title of the story refers to the efforts of the entire family, Leslie, her brother, mother and cousin to create a special welcome. At the same time Leslie's school class is given the assignment to write an essay on how to honor the servicemen (and women) of the town. Also, one of her school friends is convinced a neighbor is really a German spy. The focus is on Leslie and her situation in a small midwestern town. This is a slice of everyday life on the homefront as seen by a small girl and her family.

J435   Oppenheim, Shulamith Levey. *The Lily Cupboard.* New York: HarperCollins, 1992. 1 vol. [unpaged: 28p.]

This is mainly a picture-book with little text. Miriam, a young Jewish girl, is forced to leave her parents and hide with strangers on a farm during the German occupation of Holland. The narrative is primarily a survivor's tale since the Germans never appear although their presence is felt both in the narrative and through the pictures. This is a simple but effective story that portrays the fear and emotions of a young child.

J436   Rang, William R. *It Began With a Parachute.* Heerlandia, Alberta; Caledonia, Mich.: Inheritance Pubs., 1992. ?p.

Not seen. The Library of Congress reported that this title was cataloged under the Cataloging-in-Publication program but they had not as yet received a copy from the publisher as of March 3, 1993 (LC reply received on May 5, 1993).

J437   Rustenburg Bootsma, Paulina M. *A Mighty Fortress in the Storm.* Neerlandia, Alberta; Caledonia, Mich.: Inheritance Pubs., 1992. ?p.

Not seen. No locations on OCLC or WLN. The Library of Congress had not as yet received a copy from the publisher as of February 9, 1993.

J438 Savin, Marcia. *The Moon Bridge.* New York: Scholastic, 1992. 231p.

The story describes the life, attitudes, and friendships of several fifth graders in San Francisco after the attack on Pearl Harbor. The prejudice against Japanese-Americans is widespread in school except for some teachers and students such as Ruthie, the protagonist, who stands by her new friend, Mitzi Fujimoto. After Mitzi and her family are forced into a distant internment camp, the two girls eventually start to write to one another. At the same time, Ruthie continues to experience the irrational behavior and attitudes of her school mates over the presence of Japanese-Americans. The story concludes with the return of Mitzi and her family after the war is over and the renewal of the friendship of Ruthie and Mitzi in spite of the normal misunderstandings caused by long term separation and dramatically different experiences, particularly those of Mitzi in the camps.

INDEXES

AUTHOR INDEX

SUBJECT INDEX

WAVES (Women Accepted for
   Voluneer Emergency
   Services:
   U.S. Naval Reserve)
   J091
Women's Land Army; SEE
   British Women's Land Army

Yugoslavia
   J164

Zoos - Tokyo
   J340

TITLE INDEX

Again I See the Mountains
J304
Ahoy, Shipmate! J157
Air Patrol J046
Alan and Naomi J324
Alex, Who Won His War J414
All the Children Were Sent
Away J318
All Those Secrets of the World
J430
Aloha Means Come Back J420
Along the Tracks J415
The Animals J338
Ann Bartlett at Bataan J078
Ann Bartlett in the South Pacific
J020
Ann Bartlett Returns to the
Philippines J156
Anneliese J386
Any Old Dollars, Mister? J232
Autumn Street J344
AWOL K-9 Commando J135
Axe-time, Sword-time J316

Backwater War J305
Barry Blake of the Flying
Fortress J071
Bars on Her Shoulders J093
Bel Ria J321
The Best Kept Secret of the
War J366
The Better Part of Valour J224

Biggles Defies the Swastika
J015
Biggles Delivers the Goods
J173
Biggles Fails to Return J074
Biggles Hits the Trail J016
Biggles in Borneo J075
Biggles in the Baltic J001
Biggles in the Orient J119
Biggles in the South Seas J002
Biggles Secret Agent J003
Biggles Sees It Through J017
Biggles Sweeps the Desert J040
Black Soldier J268
Blackbird J388
Blitzcat J401
The Bolo Battalion J250
Bombardier: Tom Dixon Wins
His Wings With the Bomber
Command J081
Bomber Pilot J118
The Bombers' Moon J371
Boris J272
The Borrowed House J313
The Boy With One Shoe J225
Brian's Victory J051
The Bridge of Bombers J013
Bridge to Freedom J423
Bright Candles J300
Brother Enemy J336
Burma Rifles J208
The Burning Summer J289

About the Author

DESMOND TAYLOR is a Professor at Collins Library at the University of Puget Sound. He has published articles and books on library classification and organization, and has more recently focused on literary bibliographies. He has spent his entire career at the University of Puget Sound in various library professional positions ranging from reference and cataloging to director and archivist.

www.ingramcontent.com/pod-product-compliance
Lightning Source LLC
Chambersburg PA
CBHW070444100426

42812CB00004B/1198